10 Days

to a Sharper Memory

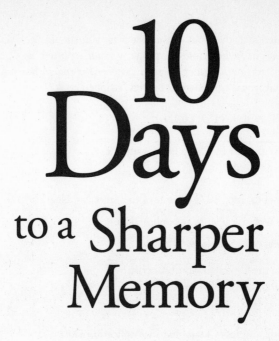

The Princeton Language Institute
and Russell Roberts

Produced by The Philip Lief Group, Inc.

WARNER BOOKS

A Time Warner Company

D0103883

WARNER BOOKS EDITION

Copyright © 2001 by Philip Lief Group Inc.
All rights reserved.

Warner Books, Inc., 1271 Avenue of the Americas, New York, NY 10020

Visit our Web site at www.twbookmark.com

A Time Warner Company

Printed in the United States of America
First Printing: July 2001
10 9 8 7 6 5 4 3 2 1

Library of Congress Cataloging-in-Publication Data
10 days to a sharper memory / [edited by] The Philip Lief Group, Inc., The
    Princeton Language Institute, and Russell Roberts.
    p. cm.
    ISBN 0-446-67666-7
    1. Mnemonics. I. Title: Ten days to a sharper memory. II. Roberts,
Russell, 1953– III. Philip Lief Group. IV. Princeton Language Institute.

BF385 .A132001
153.1'4—dc21   00-043838

Book design by Ralph Fowler
Cover design by Jon Valk

Acknowledgments

Every book is a collaborative effort. I'd like to thank Jamie Saxon and Eileen Koutnik of The Philip Lief Group for their guidance and life-saving editing skills; my wife, Patti, for helping me when things seemed impossible; and my daughter, Megan, for her constant reassurance that yes, I would get this done on time.

Contents

Day 8

Day 9

Day 10

Introduction

Do you have a "bad" memory? Do you consistently forget appointments, addresses, directions, names, and a multitude of other things? Do you constantly misplace keys, glasses, important papers . . . even the remote control for the TV? Is your forgetfulness having a negative impact on both your personal and professional life?

Would you like to stop forgetting—and start remembering?

If the answer to some or all of these questions is yes, then you've come to the right place. *10 Days to a Sharper Memory* helps turn you from absentminded and forgetful into a Memory Marvel. Unless impaired by illness or injury, a poor memory is often the result of inadequate listening skills, inefficient attention spans, and other long-ingrained bad habits. This means that your so-called bad memory can be improved—all you need are the right tools.

10 Days to a Sharper Memory introduces and explains classic memory-improving techniques, such as visualization, linking, and pegging, and then shows you how to apply them to all kinds of everyday situations, such as how to remember names and faces in a professional setting. The book also offers lifestyle tips, such as how sleep and diet affect your memory, and provides fascinating insights into the latest research as to how memory works.

Taking a step-by-step approach, *10 Days to a Sharper Memory* banishes those bad habits by showing you how to unlock the hidden power of your memory through the use of a variety of memory tools. Each day builds on the lessons and information presented in the previous day, so there is a cumulative effect in which you steadily increase your knowledge and memory tool proficiency.

So if you're tired of getting the cold shoulder from your wife and kids because you always forget their birthdays, or if you have a hard time remembering the names of people in a large group, then let *10 Days to a Sharper Memory* show you how to stop hiding from the world—and start living up to your full potential.

10
Days

to a Sharper Memory

Day 1

Getting Started
The Basic Tools of Memory

Everyone can use a better memory. Each day you're called upon to remember countless pieces of information, from where you left your wallet in the morning to a business associate's name to the key points of a report you're going to present to a new client.

Improving your memory reaps benefits in your professional, social, and personal life. Here are just a few of those benefits:

- Increase your personal success. Imagine how great it would be if you could recall facts, figures, and other important information needed at work at the drop of a hat, or rattle off financial figures from the company's last quarterly report.

- Become more successful socially. Just think, no more calling people "buddy," "honey," "kid," or "sweetheart." Remember the name of virtually everyone you meet, even in large groups.

- Become more reliable. How would it feel to remember to bring the cranberry sauce to your mother's house for

Thanksgiving dinner, rather than having to tell your mom you forgot—again. Be the one who remembers important dates, deadlines, and other information others forget.

- Save time. You actually arrive at work on time, rather than thirty minutes late, because you didn't have to spend all that time searching for your car keys. You become more efficient at work, because you don't waste time trying to remember tasks, facts, details, or paperwork.

- Learn new material quickly. With a better memory, that thick report or course textbook becomes putty in your hands, rather than a pillow for your head.

Quiz: Testing Your Memory Skills

Take the following *yes* or *no* quiz to get an accurate gauge of your memory skills:

1. Do you hit your steering wheel on the drive home from work because you forgot to make a key telephone call or to follow up with your manager on essential information she was expecting from you?

2. Do you automatically greet your spouse at the end of each day with the words "I'm sorry, I forgot to _____"?

3. Do you enlist others to help you find your keys, wallet, sunglasses, and numerous other items throughout the day?

4. Do you go through each day with the horrible feeling that you've forgotten something?

5. Do you go to the grocery store to buy milk, bread, and cheese, only to come back with soda, spaghetti, and ice

cream? (Bonus points for buying ice cream; that's *never* wrong.)

6. Have you ever gone into a room to get something, only to forget what it is, and then tried to retrace your steps, only to forget where you just were?

If you answered *yes* to more than one of these questions, your memory needs work.

Getting Started: The Basic Tools of Memory

The good news is that you don't have to be forgetful. Unlike your shoe size or height, a bad memory is not something you're born with and can't change. Unless illness or injury has affected it, you can improve your memory through training—and even have some fun along the way. By learning new behaviors and techniques, you can remember better. It's as simple as that.

Before you shake your head and say you've had a bad memory all your life and nothing can change that, consider that improving your memory hinges on just four core concepts: association, visualization, imagination, and organization. These are the building blocks of memory training. Although each is covered in greater detail in subsequent chapters, I'll introduce them briefly now so you can start thinking about them. They are the basic tools to a sharper memory for you.

- **Association.** The ability to link something that you already know with information that you need to remember. For example, taking the first letters of each of your co-workers' first names and arranging them into a common word, such as PINK (Paul, Ingrid, Nick, and Kelly).

- **Visualization.** The ability to summon a vivid, colorful picture in your mind's eye. If you need to remember to go to your hair-cutting appointment, think of Marge Simpson's huge column of blue hair stuck under a styling dryer.

- **Imagination.** The ability to let your mind roam free, thus enabling it to make outrageous associations (yes, the more outrageous the better), distinct visualizations, and a variety of other aids to help memorization. Say you have to buy spaghetti, chicken, and fresh basil at the grocery store; to jog your memory, think of the strands of spaghetti fighting the chickens in an epic battle, using the basil leaves as weapons.

- **Organization.** The ability to logically and systematically categorize information in your mind's eye. If you have trouble remembering errands, appointments, and so on, simply writing this information down in an everyday planner goes a long way toward helping your memory. But there are also ways to do this mentally.

Using Your Memory Tools

To start you thinking about the four key concepts, I'll briefly give you ideas you can use in your daily routine.

- **Association.** Next time you have to take your car for inspection remember the word LIRK. This will trigger your memory, reminding you to bring license, insurance, registration, and keys with you.

- **Visualization.** To remember a dentist appointment picture a giant toothbrush cleaning your teeth with the day of the week of your appointment painted in big white letters on the toothbrush.

- **Imagination.** Next time you need to buy a few items at the store, such as apples, blueberries, and peaches, picture each item jumping in and out of your jacket pockets and running up and down your sleeves.

- **Organization.** Buy a pocket calendar and record the top three things you have to do each week. For example, one week you may have to remember a business lunch, parent-teacher conference, and a yoga class. Reinforce this with your imagination and visualization: Picture your child's teacher in a yoga outfit sitting next to you at your business lunch.

Admittedly, if you've been suffering from memory problems all your life, at this moment it doesn't seem possible that the basic strategies represented by these four tools are ever going to help you build a sharper memory. However, by the end of this book, you will see great improvement in your memory.

A Little Bit of Trivia

Have you ever wondered where the word and concept of "memory" came from? The word "memory" has its roots in Greek mythology. According to the ancients, Mnemosyne (ni-MOS e-nee) (from whom we get the words "memory" and "mnemonic") was the goddess of memory. Mnemosyne has a forgotten history—which is ironic for the goddess of memory. She was hardly ever mentioned in mythological accounts, and consequently, almost nothing is known about her. However, she must have been quite beautiful, because even though she was the aunt of Zeus (who became ruler of the gods), he fell in love with her. Together the two of them had nine children on nine consecutive nights who became the nine Muses.

Orator, Orator

Ancient civilizations understood the value of memory. They had to, since oration was a particularly valuable skill centuries ago. Orators sometimes spoke for an extremely long time on topics of great complexity. Without paper, cards, laptop computer, TelePrompTer, or any other aid, memory was the only way an orator could remember exactly what he wanted to say.

In 1491, memory training techniques were finally exposed to a wider audience in the book *The Phoenix* by Peter of Ravenna. Other books on the subject followed, as the importance of mnemonic methods spread. Everyone from commoners to kings used memory systems. Shakespeare was supposedly a believer in mnemonic techniques. In fact, the famous Globe Theatre was called the "memory theatre."

Perhaps it was called that because an actor at this time needed a good memory in order to survive. There would be a new play every two weeks, and the current play was altered daily. There was little rehearsal, so an actor always had to be prepared. Since plays weren't meant to be published, an actor had to essentially memorize and remember his role in every play that the theatre company owned, because any one of them might be performed on any given night. In addition, an actor often played several different roles in the same play—a ghost, a soldier, a nobleman, and so on.

Let's Practice Visualization: Shakespeare 101

Don't panic; you haven't been transported, *Twilight Zone*–style, back to high school for a test on Shakespeare. Follow the instructions for the exercise below.

1. Imagine you're an actor and you have to remember the first five lines of one of the famous soliloquies from *Hamlet.*

2. Using visualization and imagination come up with ways to remember the five lines of Shakespeare below.

   > *To be, or not to be, that is the question:*
   > *Whether 'tis nobler in the mind to suffer*
   > *The slings and arrows of outrageous fortune,*
   > *Or to take arms against a sea of troubles,*
   > *And by opposing end them?*

How did you do? It's the first day, so I'll help you out a bit.

• The first line could be thought of as a buzzing pair of "two bees" with a question mark.

• For the second line, think of a "noble" brain "suffering" from a bad cold, complete with a thermometer in the mouth and watery eyes.

• The third line could be images of a "slingshot," as well as "arrows" being fired at a big dollar sign signifying "fortune."

• The fourth line could include the images of dozens of arms rising out of a stormy, or "troubled," sea.

• The fifth line is probably the most difficult; perhaps thinking of two "ends," such as the ends of a roll of salami and pepperoni, opposing each other in a duel might help.

That, of course, is a very quick and simplified use of visualization and imagery. However, it does show how the use of these techniques can work on something as difficult as recalling Shakespearean text. To try to understand why this is possible, let's take a brief trip behind the scenes to see how memory works.

Behind the Scenes: How Does Memory Work?

Let's say you need to remember your new personal identification number (PIN) for your bank card. Some research suggests that memories are recorded by electricity. Your PIN hits the synapses, the junctions that connect nerve cells with other brain cells. The cells shoot electrical signals back and forth to each other across these synapses, an activity that releases chemicals in the brain. This isn't a stop-and-go process either, like flicking a light switch on and off. With 10 billion nerve cells busily transmitting signals back and forth among 60 trillion synapses, your brain is in a constant state of supercharged activity.

Next, the PIN moves to the part of the brain cell that receives the electrical impulse, called the dendrite. Research suggests that whenever the dendrite receives an impulse, it compresses. It doesn't go back to normal until the electrical signal disappears.

Thus when you need to remember that pesky PIN, it's possible that an electrical signal deep within your brain that contains that information speeds to the appropriate location so you can retrieve it.

As to where this information is stored in the brain, this too remains a topic of great interest and conjecture. Some evidence indicates that there are specific areas in the brain for memory storage; other evidence, however, seems to support the idea that the brain is like a fragmented computer hard drive, and stores memory information in several different locations.

Memory Strategies: The Four Rs

In general, four different types of remembering are usually distinguished by memory experts: recollection, recall, recognition, and relearning. These are defined as follows:

- **Recollection.** Reconstructing events or facts based on partial clues that act as reminders, such as seeing someone who resembled your odious first boss and then thinking about him.

- **Recall.** Actively remembering something from the past, such as telling your friend that you saw someone who resembled your first boss, and her asking you, "What was his name?," which makes you think of that specific piece of information ("His name was Mr. Butters.").

- **Recognition.** Identifying previously encountered material as familiar, such as smelling onions and then remembering that Mr. Butters loved raw onion on his sandwiches.

- **Relearning.** Learning material a second time, such as pulling out the employee handbook given to you by Mr. Butters when he hired you and reading some of the important passages over again.

Although memory is often thought of as a single entity, in reality it appears as if there are two very different, very distinct, types of memories: voluntary and involuntary. For instance, the smell of cookies baking may trigger a sensation of your grandmother's kitchen without your trying to recall such a memory (that's an involuntary memory). On the other hand, if you see cookies baking, and they remind you of your grandmother's kitchen, then you might actively try to remember what her kitchen looked like (that's voluntary).

Memory Sharpener: The Long and Short of It

If all this talk about synapses, dendrites, and voluntary and involuntary function leaves your brain feeling like it's suffering a power failure, let's try simplifying things a bit by thinking of memory as having three different stages: sensory, working (also called short-term), and long-term.

- **Sensory memory.** When you first receive information, it goes into your sensory memory, where it is briefly recorded. The color of a car passing by on the highway, an unusual-looking tree, a picture in a magazine—all of these things are seen by your mind and stored in sensory memory. However, unless you do something with this material right away, it is quickly replaced by fresh sensory information.

- **Short-term (working) memory.** However, if you focus your attention on a piece of information, such as the color of that car, it may become a part of working, or short-term memory. Material in short-term memory survives longer than it does in sensory memory; from here, information is accessed and used. For example, if a friend who is an expert in chess tells you all about a special strategy that he used to win a match, the next time you play chess you may remember the name of the strategy, and possibly a few moves. However, it's doubtful that you will remember each and every move in that strategy, and carry it through the game.

- **Long-term memory.** Long-term memory, on the other hand, is much like a safe deposit box in a bank—once something is in there, it's locked up tight. It's always going to be available for use whenever necessary. Your mother's face is an example of information permanently stored in your long-term memory.

There are indications that repetition is a key factor in putting information in long-term memory. When you need it, the information is temporarily transferred or copied from long-term to short-term memory. After you're done with it, the data goes back into the vault. For instance, if you're doing a crossword puzzle, and the clue is "First U.S. President," you immediately know two things:

1. It's a really easy crossword puzzle.
2. The answer is "George Washington." You retrieve the name from long-term memory, most likely along with an image of him, probably from a history project in elementary school. Then, after answering the clue, the name goes back into long-term memory, where it is stored until the next time you need it.

Lessons from Mom: Eat Your Fruits and Vegetables!

Do you remember how your mother always used to tell you to eat your fruits and vegetables so that you'd grow up healthy and strong? While all you wanted to do was pig out on chips and other types of junk food, she was constantly ladling up steaming plates of broccoli, saying that it was good for you.

It turns out that she was right: Fruits and vegetables are good for you . . . particularly in the case of memory. (Don't you just hate it when your mother's right like that?)

Recent studies reveal that eating blueberries may help improve memory, as well as provide other health benefits. Elderly rats that ate the human equivalent of at least half a cup of blueberries a day showed improvement in balance, coordination, and short-term memory.

Blueberries, like other fruits and vegetables, contain chemicals that act as antioxidants. It is thought that antioxidants protect the body against oxidative stress, which is one of the biological processes that cause aging. But while some other fruits and vegetables, such as strawberries and spinach extract, produce memory improvements, only blueberries provide a significant impact on balance and coordination as well as memory.

Opening the Memory Tool Chest: Common Memory Obstacles

Technically, many times when you say that you can't remember something, in reality what is happening is that the information that you are trying to recall was never committed to memory in the first place. There are numerous reasons why information is not committed to memory; below are some of the most common ones:

Distraction

Following are two scenarios in which you might learn someone's name for the first time. Which do you think presents a more likely setting to trigger good memory?

Let's say that you have a young, energetic child. When you arrive to pick her up at her day-care center, nursery rhymes are coming from the tape player, an animated video is playing loudly on the TV, and a group of kids are laughing and chasing each other behind you. As your daughter jabbers excitedly to you about her day, the new day-care teacher walks up to you and introduces herself. You know you have a question you want to ask her, but you can't recall it because the Barney theme song is giving you a headache.

Now, let's say you're walking down the street on a beautiful sunny day. The birds are chirping, the air is fresh and clean, and no cars are rumbling by. Suddenly the new neighbor who just moved in down the block walks up to you and introduces herself.

Which name do you think you're more likely to remember: the first or the second?

If you said the new neighbor from example number two, you've correctly identified distraction as one of the most common stumbling blocks to a better memory. While people can do more than one thing at a time, such as chew gum while playing baseball, trying to do two things that require the same thought process (like listening to both your child and the day-care teacher) is just about impossible.

The solution is to try to eliminate distractions when you're presented with information that you want to recall. In the example of the day-care teacher, you may try walking to a quieter part of the room so you can concentrate more fully on what she says.

Lack of Focus or Concentration

If you don't focus your attention on the information you receive, it is unlikely you will retain it. For instance, you're at a party when you see someone you'd really like to meet across the room. Before you can get there, however, a friend introduces you to someone else. While shaking that person's hand, you're still thinking about meeting that other person: what you're going to say, how you look, and so on. In this situation, the odds are slim that you're going to remember the person you've just met because you're focusing on someone else. The solution, of course, is to keep your attention trained on what you're doing at the moment.

Lack of Motivation

Let's face it, if you don't consider something important, you don't concentrate on it, and consequently, you don't remember it. While not everything you encounter daily is necessary to commit to memory, being aware that important information occurs at any moment helps you to remember it. For example, you want to work on your new project idea for your boss; your boss, however, wants you to make revisions on a proposal for a new client. As you sit at your desk looking at the research you compiled for your new project idea, your boss stands in your doorway with a memo for the revisions on the proposal. You're not interested in reading the memo because your motivation is your project, not the boss's revisions.

Stress

As it does to so much else in our lives, stress also negatively affects your memory. If you're under an extreme amount of emotional or physical stress, your ability to perform auxiliary tasks such as memory is temporarily shut off or diminished. It's like when your car battery's low, and you turn on the radio when you've already got the windshield wipers and the heater going full blast; all you're likely to get is static.

Stress is also the cause of that irritating tip-of-the-tongue syndrome that we all suffer from periodically. You're trying to recall something, and it's right there, on the edge of your brain; you furrow your brow and grit your teeth, you can almost see the answer . . . yet the word or words won't come. For example, your new boss's wife is coming toward you and you draw a complete blank on her name, only remembering it rhymes with whale. Theories as to why this occurs range from the effects of age (the tip-of-the-tongue syndrome seems to occur more often as we get older) to indications that the brain stores memory information in different places (rather than just one big area labeled "memories") and that some areas deteriorate faster than others.

However, the real root cause of tip-of-the-tongue syndrome is stress. The harder you try to come up with the name of that actor on the TV show you watched last night or the brand of tea you want to recommend, the less likely it is you'll remember it.

The best way to handle this is to just relax, and either admit that you can't remember, or try to substitute another word or words. As you well know, at some point the missing word pops into your head, without your even thinking about it.

Tips to Eliminate Memory Obstacles

Here are some successful strategies to help you overcome obstacles blocking your memory:

- **Distraction.** Concentrate on the task in front of you. Tune out any possible distractor that may be around you such as other people talking, the radio, TV, video game, or computer.

- **Lack of focus or concentration.** Find a quiet place and focus on the task at hand (such as trying to remember where you put your checkbook or the perfect gift you thought of a half hour ago to buy for your friend's wedding).

- **Lack of motivation.** Clear your mind of distractions and focus on the task at hand. For example, motivate yourself to study an hour a day for an upcoming final exam and as your reward go to the movie opening with friends over the weekend.

- **Stress.** Try deep breathing exercises and visualize the task or errand being completed efficiently and accurately without any problems. (In case you don't know, deep breathing consists of slowly taking in a large amount of air and holding it in your lungs for a specified period of time. Consult your local library or the Internet for more information on deep breathing exercises.)

Tool Time: First Letter Cueing

If you find it difficult to relax, seem drawn to distractions, and have as much motivation to remember things as a gimpy horse does to run the Kentucky Derby, then a mnemonic device (remember Aunt Mnemosyne) called first letter cueing is a great place to sharpen your memory.

Typically, first letter cueing involves making an acronym out of the first letters of the words to be remembered. The most common example of this is using the acronym HOMES as an aid to remember the names of the Great Lakes (Huron, Ontario, Michigan, Erie, and Superior). Acronyms work well because you encounter them so often in daily life. Sometimes, the acronym is familiar even though the proper name is not, such as SCUBA (Self-Contained Underwater Breathing Apparatus).

Remember the saying that you learned in school to remember the notes on the lines of the treble clef: Every **G**ood **B**oy **D**eserves **F**udge? That's an example of an acrostic, which is closely related to the acronym in the first letter cueing family. Because of that saying, millions of people years out of school still remember that the notes are E, G, B, D, and F.

Acronyms and acrostics are two popular first letter cueing techniques, but the danger is that they can be forgotten as well, thus rendering their memory-jogging ability useless. To try to reduce the possibility of forgetting the acronym or acrostic, try to fix a vivid image of it in your mind.

Top Ten List: Ways to Remember Acronyms and Acrostics

Here is a list of common acronyms and acrostics. Do you remember any of these from your school days?

1. HOMES (Huron, Ontario, Michigan, Erie, and Superior).
2. SALT (Strategic Arms Limitation Talks).
3. SCUBA (Self-Contained Underwater Breathing Apparatus).
4. SONAR (Sound Navigation Ranging).
5. RAM (Random Access Memory).
6. LED (Light-Emitting Diode).
7. Every Good Boy Deserves Fudge (notes on the lines of the treble clef: E, G, B, D, F).

8. Maybe Nobody Visits Mary's Red Car (names of the New England states: Maine, New Hampshire, Vermont, Massachusetts, Rhode Island, and Connecticut).

9. Each Century Makes Progress (names of the U.S. time zones: Eastern, Central, Mountain, and Pacific).

10. Maybe Today We'll Take Fred's Sister Skating (days of the week: Monday, Tuesday, Wednesday, Thursday, Friday, Saturday, and Sunday).

Daily Tune-up: First Letter Cueing to Remember Everyday Tasks

Hopefully, by now you realize that even if your entire life has been marked by forgetfulness, it's not too late to reverse that pattern. So let's put your newfound confidence to the test by attempting one simple task via first letter cueing. Let's try something basic, like remembering to set the alarm clock tonight so that you wake up on time tomorrow. Using first letter cueing, let's devise the following acronym: Set Clock Alarm Now. Thus, the acronym is SCAN. Now repeat the word "scan" over and over to fix it in your mind.

To further increase your chances of remembering, conjure up a visual image to go with the acronym. One example of a basic image is a scanner that records prices, like at the supermarket checkout line. If you want, you can also picture an alarm clock being passed over the scanner. Now the mental picture of an alarm clock being scanned should remind you of SCAN, and you will remember to set your alarm.

You can also make the mental picture more vivid. For instance, instead of a price scanner, you might picture Mr. Spock from the *Star Trek* series. He was always "scanning" things (aliens, planets, and so on). Now, picture Spock sitting atop your alarm clock. Although the image is somewhat absurd, that's exactly the idea—the more outlandish the image, the less likely you are to forget it.

Pop Quiz: Devising Acronyms

Before you close the memory tool chest for this first day, let's see if you can come up with acronyms for the following five evening tasks:

1. Brushing your teeth
2. Putting out the cat
3. Paying the bills
4. Taking out the trash
5. Turning off the lights

Finished? Good. Remember, no acronym is wrong. However, here are some suggestions:

1. Brushing your teeth: TEN (Teeth Every Night—and if you do, you'll have a perfect "10" smile; think of your gleaming white teeth with a big number 10 on them).

2. Putting out the cat: CON (Cat Outside Now—think of how cats are such con artists anyway, and this one's easy).

3. Paying the bills: POT (Pay On Time—and a pot is all you're going to have left if you don't remember to pay your bills on time).

4. Putting out the trash: GO (Garbage Out—think of a garbage can being tagged out at home plate in a baseball game).

5. Turning off the lights: LOAN (Lights Out At Night— summon up a mental picture of you forking over a huge

bag of money, complete with a $ on it, to the electric company to pay for leaving the lights on all night).

Tip of the Day: Sleep and Memory

Here's a memory tip that might jolt your brain awake: If you want to remember something, fall asleep.

No, don't doze off right in the middle of the supermarket if you can't remember what items you were supposed to pick up. Rather, there is evidence that suggests falling asleep immediately after learning something helps you to retain the information better. Timing is everything, however; if you're too tired the information won't make an impression, whereas if you're too awake the material will snap your eyelids open like one of those cartoon eyeshades. The material that you're trying to remember also has to be easily comprehended; you're not going to be able to read the Theory of Relativity right before bed and wake up ready to cover a blackboard with equations.

But the next time you need to remember something, try doing it right before you get some shut-eye. You may wake up and find yourself not only refreshed, but with a better memory as well.

By the way, there is no evidence to support the popular notion that you can learn and remember while sound asleep. Anything that you do retain probably happened during a period of wakefulness. All you're really doing by playing those learning tapes while you sleep is educating your pillow.

Congratulations! Now you've successfully completed Day 1 of this ten-day process on improving your memory. Along the way you've gained some confidence that you can do it, along with background information, and a few memory-helping techniques to get you started. That wasn't too hard, was it?

Now that both you and your memory are warmed up, you're going to move on to ways you can remember one of the most important facets of life—names and faces.

Day 2

Names and Faces, Part I

On a daily basis you encounter many individuals, some of whom you've never met before. Whether you're at work, school, social situations, and so on, remembering names and faces is not always easy. This chapter introduces surefire tips, strategies, and exercises for committing names and faces to your memory.

Terror at a Cocktail Party

You're at a chic cocktail party where you hope to make important new business contacts. You've spent more money than you earn in a month on a new outfit and you've perfected the art of small talk to the point that witty comments fall effortlessly from your mouth like gold nuggets. You're primed and ready to make a good impression.

Suddenly, from across the room, you see someone familiar, some corporate bigwig that you met once—but her name escapes you! Desperately you bob and weave among the other partygoers as she approaches, trying to hide until you can think of her name and avoid the ultimate embarrassment. But it's no good, she's coming toward you. You quickly look away hoping she didn't see you. Too late, she's standing right in front of you with her hand extended and a smile on her face.

"Hello, John," she says. "Nice to see you again." A large group of nearby partygoers (most of whom can't remember her name either) turn to you expectantly.

As a silent scream wells up in your throat, you extend your hand and say, "Hello— you!"

What's Your Name?

If you're lucky, forgetting someone's name happens in a relaxed, informal setting, and no damage is done. However, if luck deserts you, you forget a name in the middle of the most important business meeting of your life. The next day you find yourself at the company's northernmost field office.

If you have a tendency to forget names, don't despair; just as in other areas of memory improvement, there are mnemonic techniques you can learn to dramatically enhance your ability to remember names.

Of course, the basic question is: Why can you remember a face so easily, but yet forget the name that goes with that face? The answer may have to do with how the brain obtains and stores information. Some scientists believe that the brain stores memories of faces in a different area than it does memories of names, or the memories of other objects. For instance, when you look at a couch, your brain remembers it for its functionality, or feel, just as it does for a wristwatch, an automobile, or hundreds of other items. However, when you see a face, your brain is summoning that information from a different region. When a name is required to go with the face, that information is in yet a third area.

When you see a familiar face, you recognize it, just like you recognize a couch or wristwatch. However, to remember the name that goes with the face requires *recall* (remember it's one of the four Rs you learned in Day 1)—a much more difficult task for the brain. For example, if the couch you *recognized* had a specific label, you would probably find it as difficult to *recall* that name as you would the name of a person that you *recognized*. The brain finds it much easier to recognize things than it does to recall them.

Of course, knowing that doesn't help you when you forget a name in an awkward situation. In an increasingly impersonal world, a person's name has assumed monumental importance. Each day, you are asked to identify yourself more and more by a monotonous succession of digits: Social Security number, ATM number, telephone number, and so on. Amid the dreary similarity of all these numbers, your name reminds you of your individuality, and makes you different from anyone else. Thus people often get offended when their name is forgotten.

So how do you avoid forgetting names or, better yet, how do you *remember* names, and place them with faces?

Verbal Association: Say It, Say It, and Say It Again

Fortunately, in addition to paying attention, there are mnemonic strategies to help you link names with faces. Basically, these involve both visual and verbal methods. Let's take a look at three ways to remember names:

1. **Repeat right away.** For instance, if Bill Davenport introduces himself to you, immediately repeat the name

to yourself mentally. (This, of course, forces you to pay attention to the name.)

2. **Comment on the name.** For example, if you've ever known anyone named Davenport in your life, you might say, "Bill Davenport. A family named Davenport used to live near my parents in lower Bucks County. Are you related to them?"

3. **Use the name again as soon as possible, and repeat it out loud.** After exchanging greetings and some small talk with Bill you could turn to someone else you know and say, "Kathy, I'd like you to meet Bill Davenport."

Visual Association: A Picture Paints a Person's Name

Using the three-step strategy just described will significantly improve your memory for names and faces. However, you may think, it's the mnemonic equivalent of eating just one potato chip: You want more!

You may, for example, find it easier to process information visually rather than verbally. That explains why the face-name association memory strategy was developed. It utilizes the following three steps:

1. Link the name with something real.

2. Identify distinctive features of the person's face.

3. Visually associate the name with the person's facial feature.

Sounds easy, doesn't it? That's the beauty of the face-name association strategy—it *is* easy. Hopefully, after learning this, your days of calling people "sport," "sweetheart," "buddy," and "pal," because you don't know their real names and are too embarrassed to admit it, will be over. Let's examine the first step—linking—in detail.

Linking

When you link a name with something real, you are laying the groundwork to commit that name to memory. It's an important tool in your memory tool chest.

Link words by placing a name with an image. Say you've just been introduced to Jennifer Goodwin; her last name easily links to a "good win" by your favorite sports team, such as the New York Yankees, the Denver Broncos, or even your child's soccer team. Repeat the association in your mind until it's clear. Now, whenever you encounter and recognize Jennifer, a mental image of your favorite team engaged in a "good win" should come to mind, and so should Jennifer's last name.

Of course, Goodwin was an easy example, because the name so readily links to a common term. Let's try a more difficult name, such as Oppenheim. I already see you shaking your head, saying to yourself, "There's no way that links up with anything!"

But it does, if you open the doors of your mind's eye. Oppenheim could easily be "Open Home" ("Oppen" = "Open" and "Heim" = "Home"). You don't have to go for an exact match, just something that's close and that triggers the linking association and a visual image in your brain. By the same token, the name "Houlihan" could become "hold a hand," or even "hooligan."

It's better to pick concrete objects or terms to link with, though, rather than abstract concepts. For example, linking someone with a concept like "grumpy" or "aloof" won't work if the person didn't act like that. Then you might wind up knowing that person only by the last name of "Mr. Grumpy."

It's also not a good idea to pick celebrity links. This is because the image of the celebrity can be so strong that it often overshadows the nonfamous name, so that if you meet somebody that you've previously linked as "Harrison Ford," all you think of is the famous actor and not the person in front of you.

As you've probably figured out by now, linking also works with first names. "Hairy" for Harry, "microphone" for Mike, "dollar" for "Bill," and so on. One advantage with devising links for first names is that the more you use them, the more they become embedded in your long-term memory, and pop out almost without your thinking about it.

Exercise: Do It Your Way

Now it's your turn. Below are ten first and last names; match each name with the appropriate link.

1. Arnold		a.	Eat a ton
2. Barson		b.	Mitt shell
3. Eaton		c.	Hog's land
4. Hoagland		d.	Roads
5. James		e.	Wit acre
6. Loftin		f.	All tuckered out
7. Mitchell		g.	Jams; aims
8. Rhodes		h.	Arm old
9. Tucker		i.	Left in; loft
10. Whitaker		j.	Son of bar, bar's son
11. Jackie		k.	Rob her
12. Philip		l.	Fill up
13. Adam		m.	Add 'em
14. Robert		n.	Jack; key

ANSWERS: 1 h, 2 j, 3 a, 4 c, 5 g, 6 i, 7 b, 8 d, 9 f, 10 e, 11 n, 12 l, 13 m, 14 k

Very good. Now look at the list again and make up your own link. Since there are no right or wrong answers, as long as you come up with a link—any link, and not just those listed—then congratulate yourself on a job well done.

Open the Memory Tool Chest: Advanced Linking

As you know, often one tool by itself is not enough to do the job. By the same token, sometimes tools have to be augmented in order to do what you need them to do. For instance, trying to use a manual screwdriver to drive screws into wood or metal without predriven holes is going to be a long and difficult job. However, if you augment that screwdriver with electricity, then the work goes quicker and easier.

It's the same thing with your memory tools. By itself, the linking tool is excellent in many respects. However, in order to use it to match name and face recognition with such personal details such as occupation or titles, it needs to be augmented. So open your memory tool chest, and dig around—don't prick your finger on the sharp humor tool—until you find an item called advanced linking.

Advanced linking is simply taking the linking technique that you've previously learned to the next level. How do you do this? By making a title, occupation, or other important detail part of the mental picture that you create for a person. Let's once again trot out our old friend John Fox. If he is a dentist, then you can add toothbrushes to the foxes that you've already pictured pouring out of his large ears. If he is a law enforcement officer, then those foxes should be wielding night sticks. If he has a military title, then putting a military uniform on those foxes should be enough to trigger the association in your memory.

You can also use advanced linking to add other bits of personal details to the mental picture. Say that Dr. John Fox loves to play golf; what, then, would be more logical than having those toothbrush-waving foxes swinging golf clubs? If he enjoys jogging, then placing running shoes on the feet of those foxes should be more than sufficient to trigger your memory. As you can see, using advanced linking enables you to remember a considerable amount of information about a person.

Remember that it takes a lot longer to explain this technique than it does to actually practice it. Once you get in the habit of using this memory tool, it will become second nature, and the mental pictures will spring to mind quickly and easily. And if you're worried about your mind becoming cluttered up with so many zany mental pictures that it looks like a kaleidoscope changing colors, stop fretting; after you use this information a few times, it will become part of your knowledge base, and the mental picture will fade.

Exercise: What Color Are Their Parachutes?

This exercise is a fun takeoff on the famous career-planning book *What Color Is Your Parachute?* Try to determine the professions or personal details about the following people, based on the mnemonic clues given below (hint—sometimes I've included a profession and a hobby or refer to a professional title):

1. A woman with dozens of colorful, cut flowers sprouting from every inch of her clothing.

2. A man with baseball bats wearing stethoscopes protruding from his ears.

3. A woman whose glasses bear the image of *Star Trek*'s immortal James T. Kirk.

4. A man with tractors pouring out of his shirt pocket.

5. A woman with rulers and blackboards plastered all over her cheeks.

> ANSWERS: 1 a florist, 2 a doctor who is also a baseball fan, 3 a woman who has the title "Captain" in her name, 4 a farmer, 5 a teacher

As you can see, advanced linking is the type of tool that gives your memory a leg-up on everyone else.

Memory Sharpener: Imagine That

Remember the discussion in Day 1 on imagination, and how important it is for improving your memory? Now you're going to apply this technique to further sharpen your name-face memory skills.

If linking is an important tool in your memory tool chest, then think of imagery as a maintenance device that keeps this tool clean, sharp, and ready to perform at peak efficiency.

Using imagery in association with remembering names and faces further cements the person's name in your mind. For instance, if you're introduced to Dr. Lawrence Morgan, you might immediately link Morgan with "mortgage" to help you remember the name. As for the "Dr.," why not imagine him wearing a stethoscope, or wearing a white hospital coat with a thermometer sticking out of the top pocket. The next time you see this man, the image of the stethoscope helps you remember that he is a doctor.

You can do the same for other titles. For a judge, picture the person wearing a long black robe or holding a gavel. For religious titles, such as "Reverend," "Father," or "Rabbi," imagine the individual holding an article emblematic of their faith, such as a Bible or Torah. Think of people with military titles such as "Colonel" or "Captain" wearing their uniforms.

Daily Tune-up: Mental Imagery Without a Net

Now here's another tip, one that will keep your imagination tool honed to razor-sharpness: Use humor and exaggeration to improve and enhance your mental imagery.

Using humor and exaggeration even works with titles. For a military title such as "Colonel," don't just picture the person in uniform; picture a uniform with huge medals on the chest and giant stars jutting out from the shoulders. Perhaps you can put a GI helmet on the person, or even have him poking his helmeted head out of the top of a fierce-looking tank. A physician doesn't have to have just a plain old stethoscope, but rather a gigantic stethoscope that sticks out of his ears and encircles his head like a bizarre halo.

If you're thinking that you can't do this, that you lost your ability to exaggerate and be humorous the day you decided that you were all grown up, think again; just like your memory, your imagination has been gathering cobwebs because you haven't tried to use it for years. All it needs is a little kick start to get it going again.

Practice: Ten Names to Challenge Your Mental Imagery

How can you use humor and exaggeration to increase your mental imagery for ten of the names you developed links for earlier in the chapter? Let's try:

1. For Arnold ("Arm old"), think of a man with a very old arm, possibly resembling Father Time with a long white beard and walking in a hunched-over fashion.

2. For Barson ("Son of bar, bar's son"), picture a person holding a large, adult-sized bar or barbell in one hand and in the other hand a smaller, kid-sized version of the same.

3. For Eaton ("Eat a ton"), think of that person sitting hungrily with a knife and fork at a large table literally overflowing with food.

4. For Hoagland ("Hog's land"), picture a person standing in a pleasant green field, with the sun shining, that is just jammed with hogs—so many hogs, in fact, that they're even standing atop one another just to be able to look around. Put quizzical looks on the faces of the hogs to show that they're just as perplexed by all of them in this field as you are.

5. For James ("Jams, aims"), visualize a person looking at row upon row of bottled jam, which are lining endless shelves at the supermarket. Picture the bottles with faces straining for some elbow room, and pushing thin little arms out to try to make some space between them.

6. For Loftin ("Left in, loft"), think of a hayloft in an old, drafty barn, in which a beautiful farm boy or farm girl is reclining.

7. For Mitchell ("Mitt shell"), picture a person holding a baseball glove, such as a catcher's mitt, that's entirely made out of seashells. To make the image even more memorable, picture the mit of shells as being shattered by a baseball that has just been caught. Imagine the shell pieces flying into the air and clattering down onto the floor.

8. For Rhodes ("Roads"), think of a person looking at a long, endless string of roads all going this way and that, just like one of those cartoon images where the roads are so confusing that they wind up tied into a knot with a pretty pink bow.

9. For Tucker ("All tuckered out"), imagine someone sleeping soundly in bed. Perhaps he's wearing one of those large, striped nightcaps like you always see in Dickens illustrations, and over his head is a picture of sheep jumping over a fence (to illustrate that he's counting sheep to fall asleep).

10. For Whitaker ("Wit acre"), think of a person watching a large parcel of ground laughing. For extra effect, give the ground the face of a famous comedian, such as Groucho Marx, complete with huge, black greasepaint mustache and thick black eyebrows.

The Name Game

Here are two ideas to help you practice verbal and visual association:

1. The next time you drop your child off at school, devise a link and visualization for each of his classmates.

2. Here's a chance to put your newly developed linking
   and visualizing ability to the test. The next time you
   read a newspaper or magazine article, try to think of
   links and visualizations for each name in the story.

Pop Quiz: Terror at a Cocktail Party II

Hard to believe that there's a sequel to the first "Terror at a
Cocktail Party." Six months after your debacle at the first
cocktail party, you've managed to find your way back to a
semblance of professional respectability. You've even managed
to get invited to another important cocktail party.

As you're standing at the party, sparkling water in hand,
your good friend Amy comes up to you and says: "Here's
someone I'd like you to meet." Then she turns to a woman
standing beside her and says, "This is Lesley Mariposa. She's
in charge of purchasing and outside vendor contracts at our
Arizona office."

What do you do now?

A. Whisper to Amy, "Don't tell me her name, I'll just for-
   get it."
B. Make a joke about her name.
C. Repeat the name mentally to yourself.

If your answer was "C," congratulate yourself on paying attention to what you've read so far. Now what?

A. Comment on the name in some manner, such as, "Oh,
   what a lovely name—Mariposa is Spanish for butterfly,
   isn't it?"
B. Say, "Speaking of outside vendor contracts, how about
   we meet next week to discuss it further?"

C. Shake hands with her and say, "It's nice to meet you."

If your answer was "A," then not only have you been paying attention to what you've been reading, but you're also comprehending it. But now the pressure's on; having gotten the first two questions right, what do you do next to ensure that you remember her name the next time?

A. Take out a pen and write it on your hand.
B. Ask her if she's the same "Lesley Mariposa" who had a fender-bender with your therapist on the corner of Maple and Sioux avenues yesterday.
C. Introduce her to someone else at the party, making certain that you repeat her name out loud as soon as possible.

If you answered "C," then you've taken a giant step in improving your ability to remember names.

Lessons from Mom: I Told You to Stop Listening to That Music!

Remember when you and your mother argued about music? When you were a kid, you, of course, wanted to listen to your type of music—rock 'n' roll, rap, heavy metal, country, whatever. Your mother's reaction to this was probably similar to that of a person having four wisdom teeth extracted without novocaine; she ranted and raved and told you how your music was no good for you. Why don't you listen to some *real* music, she probably said, like big band or classical. You scoffed, and merrily went on your head-banging way—but she was right. Again!

Researchers have found that the IQs of college students

went up nine points after ten minutes of listening to classical music. Studies performed at the University of California at Irvine showed that students did better on IQ tests after hearing ten minutes of Mozart's Sonata for Two Pianos in D Major (there are even *Mozart for Babies* CDs now).

The bad news is that the intelligence increase only lasts about fifteen minutes, so those of you who were planning to become new Einsteins by rushing out and buying every classical CD you could lay your hands on can just relax. However, this is a promising new research field, with great potential. Maybe someday in the future, when you want to help improve your memory, all you'll have to do is slip some soothing Mozart into the CD player—just like Mom told us to do so many years ago.

Tip of the Day

Here's a fishy idea: To help boost your brain power, turn to our finny friends—not for eating, but watching.

Does "watching" mean that you have to spend hours staring at your fish tank? No, in this instance "watching" means just observing fish in the tank. It's all part of stimulating your brain, which some researchers believe leads to better memory abilities.

According to studies, brain cells that are stimulated are larger and healthier than those that are not, leading to an increase in brain activity. Similar to muscles in the body, the brain needs activity to stimulate, or "exercise" it.

Thus, researchers suggest filling your environment with fish tanks, colorful walls, curtains and fabrics, books, music, and even a shortwave radio that can pick up broadcasts from around the world. Even putting a birdhouse or bird feeder outside the window exercises your brain by making it look at and record the different types of birds that the feeder attracts.

In short, any type of activity that forces the brain to focus, concentrate, and think is a good exercise. There is also evidence indicating that stimulating brain cells can stop them from shrinking with age, thus reversing the decline in memory function and ability that often bedevils people as they age. So to remember better, make life more interesting for your brain.

Take a deep breath; you completed Day 2 with flying colors. In this chapter you added several new tools to your tool chest, including how to remember names and faces by building on the knowledge you gleaned over the last couple of days. Don't think you're done with names and faces, though. They appear again in Day 3 along with new tools and techniques to help you master names quickly and easily.

Day 3

Names and Faces,
Part II

Think fast. What would you do if you walked into a business meeting, armed with the memory tools to remember names and faces that you learned in Day 2, and the first person you were introduced to was a man named Peter Esposito? Is there a way to remember names that don't immediately suggest a link and/or visualization? Yes. Relax, refocus your eyes, and—most important—don't blame Mr. Esposito. Believe it or not, there are mnemonic tools you can use to remember his name and those of all his relatives, if you really needed to. If you think that's impossible, it's not.

Open the Memory Tool Chest:
Difficult Names

First, dig out two key tools you already have—linking and visualization—to remember seemingly difficult names. Also, grab the humor tool as well, and make sure that it's sharp. Now you're ready to tackle the job.

Let's start by considering the name "Esposito." When you

first hear it you might think, "There's no way to link and visualize that"—but there is.

1. Divide the name into syllables.
2. Pronounce each one: "Es-poh-zee-toh." (If you've been introduced to him you know how the name is pronounced.)
3. Substitute "expose" for "Es-poh" and "a-toe" for "zee-toh" and you've got a link: Peter "Expose-a-toe."

The next step is to come up with a visualization—and remember, the more comical or outrageous, the better. For "Expose-a-toe," imagine an oversized toe in a bright red sock sticking out of a hole in a shoe.

Let's try another name. (Pay attention because you're going to get a chance to do this on your own very soon.) You've just been introduced to your spouse's new supervisor, Mary Czarnecki. To come up with a link for this name, listen closely to the pronunciation: "Zar-NECK-ee." If you listen carefully, then the linking words should come to you fairly quickly, because they're very similar to the pronunciation: "Zar-NECK-ee." As for a visualization, how about a ruler like a czar or a king with a prominent neck that's covered with a giant letter "e"? Picture in your mind a very dignified-looking man, possibly with a beard and monocle and maybe even wearing a crown, all dressed up in fancy clothes, with a large, bulging neck that's festooned with a huge, brightly colored letter "e." That'll do it. You're set. The more vivid and exaggerated the visualization, the more likely it will be to stick like chewing gum in your mind.

Exercise: Practice Links and Visualization for Last Names

Now it's your turn. Below are five uncommon last names. Come up with a link and visualization for each one (the links that follow will help you with the pronunciation). Remember, don't try to make the link exactly fit the name—if you come up with something similar, your memory and common sense takes over to fill in the rest accurately.

1. Gresavage
2. Kalnitsky
3. Nowacki
4. Trombly
5. Winstanley

Time's up! Pencils down. How did you do? Although there are "answers" below, remember that no link or visualization is wrong if it works for you. Try these on for size:

1. **Gresavage.** "Gray-savage." Picture a caveman or other savage creature in a fashionable gray pinstriped suit, perhaps with a colorful tie and handkerchief sticking out of the breast pocket.

2. **Kalnitsky.** "Cal-knits-skis." Imagine Cal using gigantic knitting needles to "knit" a pair of skis out of a pile of wood, the same way someone would knit a baby's blanket or an afghan. For an extra touch, picture Cal sweating mightily, tongue sticking out of his mouth in concentration, as he struggles to "knit" his skis.

3. **Nowacki.** "No-whack-E." Picture a large letter "E," with a boy's head, lying across his father's lap about to get a spanking, and shouting "No."

4. **Trombly.** "Tromp-glee." Here the visualization can be a mammoth foot about to tromp (step on) the word "glee." To make the image more vivid, put a worried face on the word "glee" as it looks at the huge foot looming over it.

5. **Winstanley.** "Win-Stanley." For this visualization, imagine a man named Stanley just crossing the finish line in a race, or else being carried off the field on his teammates' shoulders.

Added Bonus

Although it is possible to come up with links and associations for almost every name, nothing in this world is absolute: Once in a while, you're going to encounter a name that simply does not lend itself to this technique. No matter how hard you try to use your memory tools they just won't work. Like trying to figure out how to program a VCR, all your efforts go for naught, and you're left with an immense feeling of frustration.

For instance, say you've tried and tried to come up with a visualization for Mr. Mzyplitlikz. Try as you might, however, you can't devise a single image, and the pronunciation of the name ("miz-plit-LIK-zee") is no help either. Have your memory tools failed you? Absolutely not. After all, didn't you keep seeing this man in your mind's eye as you struggled and strained to come up with a visualization? Because of all that effort, it's extremely likely that the next time you see this gentleman, his name will come to you.

But there's a bonus: All the effort you put into trying to come up with a link and association helps you remember that name. Just like after struggling for an hour putting your kid's "easy assembly" Christmas toy together you'll always remember it, you will also remember the rare name that defies all links and associations.

Tool Time, Part 1: Features

In case you haven't noticed it by now, your memory toolbox is quite large, and capable of holding an awful lot of mnemonic tools, techniques, and strategies. Take a moment now and rummage around in there; so far you should have tools for visualization and linking, a humor tool, and one for first letter cueing. Now it's time to add another tool for remembering names and faces: using features.

Think of Paul Newman. What's the first thing about him that comes to mind? Is it his hands, his ears, or his nose? If any of those *does* come to mind, you've got the wrong guy; Paul Newman's distinctive facial feature is his sparkling blue eyes. By the same token, what do you think of when you hear the name Whoopi Goldberg? Most likely it's her unique hairstyle.

Noticing the distinctive facial features or characteristics of a person is another mnemonic tool for helping you remember his or her name. And, just like the prize in a box of Cracker Jack, there's an extra bonus that comes with using this technique—it forces you to look at and concentrate on the person's face when you first meet him or her. Remember from Day 1 that concentration was identified as one of the keys to a sharper memory power? The features and characteristics tool also helps improve your focus and concentration.

Celebrity Quotient: Famous Facial Features

Below are the names of six famous people. Immediately write down or say the first feature that comes to mind when you see the name:

1. Julia Roberts

2. Barbra Streisand

3. Jay Leno

4. Cindy Crawford

5. Lauren Hutton

6. John Travolta

What did you come up with? Most likely it was Roberts's smile, Streisand's prominent nose, Leno's lantern jaw, Crawford's mole on her face, Hutton's space between her front teeth, and Travolta's cleft chin.

All of these are distinctive facial features that immediately spring to mind when the image of that person pops into your head. Although you haven't thought about it in this context until now, these distinct features have actually been functioning like memory tools, enabling you to recall the celebrities' names and faces.

The same principle holds true when using this memory tool as an aid for remembering names and faces of everyday people. First impressions are often the most lasting, and what strikes you about a face now is what's most likely to strike you the next time you see it. That's the beauty of this system; it works for you, and you alone. What you choose about the face can be anything, from the hair all the way down to the chin, or all the way over to the very tips of the earlobes. Just try to make sure that it's a standout feature, something that you notice immediately upon meeting the person. The following top ten list should help you choose your reminder.

Top Ten List: Distinctive Things to Notice About a Face

1. **Hair.** Long, short, thick, thin, curly, or straight? Is the hair so clean and luxurious that you want to bathe in it, or is there so little of it that you're not even sure the person has hair?

2. **Forehead.** Narrow, wide, or high? Is the forehead smooth and broad, or is it full of lines and furrows?

3. **Eyebrows.** Straight, arched, or bushy? Is each eyebrow separate and distinct, or are they crashing into each other over the nose to give the person a head start on their werewolf impersonation?

4. **Eyes.** Narrow, wide-spaced, or close-set? Are the eyes as warm and friendly as your grandmother's, or as cold and distant as an IRS agent's at audit time?

5. **Nose.** Long, short, fat, or thin? Is the nose as small and pert as a Barbie doll's, or long and large like a ski jump at the Olympics?

6. **Nostrils.** Flaring, wide, or narrow? Are the nostrils as delicate and fluted as a young girl's, or pinched like Ebenezer Scrooge's?

7. **Cheeks.** Full or sunken? Are the cheekbones so high and sharp that you could hang a picture on them, or so low and hollow that you could hide buried treasure in them?

8. **Lips.** Straight, big, pouting, or thick? Are the lips as full and pouty as Marilyn Monroe's, or as thin and sharp as a razor blade?

9. **Chin.** Cleft, receding, or prominent? Does the chin fill out the rest of the face nicely and unobtrusively, or does

it stick out so far it should have a red warning light on it so that passing airplanes don't strike it?

10. **Ears.** Close to or far out from the head? Do the ears lie flat or do they stick out so far the person could beat Dumbo in a race of flying elephants?

Tool Time, Part 2: Characteristics

Here's another tool to put in your memory tool chest for remembering names: the unusual characteristic.

An unusual characteristic can be glasses, a striking item of clothing such as a bow tie or brightly striped sweater, a distinctive piece of jewelry such as earrings, or anything else that marks that person in your mind's eye. For instance, what's the first thing you think of when you hear the name "Elton John"? For most people it's the outrageous glasses that he wears. Similarly, the name "George Burns" immediately calls to mind his ever-present cigar, while Groucho Marx will always be remembered for his eyebrow wiggle and Charlie Chaplin for his cane and derby.

As you can see, identifying unusual characteristics comes in handy when trying to remember the names that are important to you. If there is nothing distinctive about the person's face, use glasses, jewelry, clothing, or anything else that strikes you as distinctive and unusual—just like Elton John's glasses. Again, whatever you choose serves you, and you alone, and that's why it works.

All Together Now—Associate!

It's now time to associate everything we've learned about names and faces together. Remember to have your humor tool sharpened and ready as well! Let's go back to our buddy Peter Esposito. If you remember, our link for his last name was "Expose-a-toe" and our visualization was an oversized toe in a bright red sock sticking out of a hole in a shoe.

Now take another look at Peter. The unusual facial feature or distinctive characteristic that he possesses is a pair of eyeglasses. A mental picture you can draw is one in which an oversized big toe, jutting out of a tear in a bright red sock, is hanging off the side of a pair of glasses. Another image can be dozens of those same naked toes sticking out of that pair of glasses.

For Nowacki, or "No-whack-E," you had as your visualization a large letter "E," in the shape of a boy, lying across his father's lap about to get a spanking, and shouting "No." However, perhaps Ms. Nowacki is wearing large gold hoop earrings. Just picture those poor "E's" lying inside those giant earrings, swinging back and forth as they're crying "No." And as for Mr. Trombly ("Tromp-glee"), who has a very high forehead, picture that huge foot that you had visualized clomping about his forehead, trying to step on that poor helpless "glee."

Now you (who used to be so "bad" at remembering names that even your wife and children had to wear name tags) can remember scores of names. Although at first it may seem odd to you to try to come up with a link, visualization, and mental picture for each name, you'll soon find yourself doing it automatically. By associating all of these techniques, you'll find that your memory for names and faces will stop resembling Swiss cheese, and start resembling an iron safe.

Helpful Hints on Remembering Names and Faces

Here are a few more points to help you master the art of using your memory to remember names and faces:

- If you meet several new people in a row or in a short space of time, it's important to try to review each mental picture as soon as possible, to lodge them firmly in your mind. For example, if you're using this technique at a business conference, use the break between presentations or workshops to review your links and visualizations.

- If you know in advance that you're going to be meeting several new people at once, try meeting them in different settings. For example, try meeting some people gathered in a conversation and others waiting in line for food or beverages. This not only makes each meeting unique, but also gives you time to fix your mental picture in your head.

- Above all, have fun with these memory tools! Use each occasion to give your imagination free rein, to let it roam over the landscape of your mind and come up with the most vivid, funny picture you can conjure up. Make a game of it, and keep trying to top your last effort. If you do, reward yourself—you've earned it!

Magazine Madness

Here's a way to practice making mental pictures that you can do with your whole family or a group of friends. Choose a magazine that contains a lot of photos, and select pictures such as those that appear in advertisements with ordinary people or models (not celebrities or supermodels that go by only one name like Madonna or Naomi). Assign one of the following tasks to a different member of your family. For each clipping, have someone:

A. Invent a name

B. Devise a link

C. Name the prominent facial feature or distinctive characteristic

D. Develop a visualization

You can also do all these steps yourself. Once you have the above four pieces of information, your next task is to come up with a mental picture for each person. But don't treat this exercise like *Mission: Impossible:* Have fun with it!

Memory Sharpener: Built-in Imagery

Have you ever noticed how some things in life have the perfect name? For instance, the word "television" just seems to ideally describe that device. Other possible names, such as VisionoScope, Picture Box, or Motionatron, just don't seem to fit.

It's the same way with some names. Certain names instantly conjure up a perfect image in your mind—an image that can be used to remember the name. This is called built-in imagery.

How does built-in imagery work? Easily. For example, if someone introduces himself to you now as "John Fox," what do you immediately think of? That's right, a fox. A person with the last name of "Gardner" should remind you of gardening, while "Catherine Knott" should summon up an image of a rope tied in a thick knot and "Wally Canter" should summon up an image of a horse cantering.

Of course, once you come up with the mental image you still must link it with something in order to impress it upon your memory. Just because John Fox's last name is the same as a common animal will probably not be enough to enable you to recall it when necessary. Thus built-in imagery is most effective when used with the other mnemonic techniques you've learned, such as humor, exaggeration, and the use of facial characteristics.

For instance, let's take a look again at John Fox. If his most distinguishing characteristic is his large ears, then picture foxes scurrying out of his ears. To make the image even more memorable, have them pouring out of his ears in a virtual fox hunt, and running all about his face as if they're being chased by the most determined pack of bloodhounds this side of Merrie Olde England.

Remember Catherine Knott? Her most memorable facial characteristic is a rather pronounced chin; when you look at her, you can see knots of rope skiing down her chin. Wally Canter wears thick glasses; picture him riding a cantering horse with huge black glasses.

Exercise: What's in a Name?

Below are ten names with built-in imagery. A distinguishing facial feature or characteristic of the person is also listed. Come up with an image and a link to remember each name.

- Warren Stone (bald)
- Phyllis White (large nose)
- Marcia Rabbit (prominent front teeth)
- George Cliff (sad eyes)

- Arthur Brown (wears bow ties)
- Danielle Dock (wears colorful scarves)
- Paul Beach (wears glasses)
- Bill Birch (well-lined forehead)
- Sarah Butler (high cheekbones)
- Edward Porter (smokes pipe)

Pop Quiz: What's in a Name, Part 2

Let's challenge your imagination in reverse now. Below are ten descriptions of people developed via built-in imagery and distinguishing features. Can you guess what their last names are merely from the descriptions alone?

1. A man with pieces of shrubbery growing out of his eyebrows.
2. A man with the words "Stop," "Yield," and "Merge" printed on his forehead.
3. A woman with long, flat pieces of wood jutting out from her glasses.
4. A man with sewing needles, measuring tape, and thread spools coming out of his ears.
5. A woman with drapes hanging down from a rod balanced on the bridge of her nose.
6. A woman with gray, doglike animals prowling about on her brightly colored sweater.
7. A man whose cheekbones are loaded with small pieces of bread.
8. A man with sprinklers jumping about his bald head.
9. A woman surrounded by knights in shining armor from medieval times.

10. A man with people in white uniforms and tall white hats taking loaves of bread and pastries from a large brick oven.

So how did you do? Did you guess them all, or at least some of them? Remember that it isn't important if you got them all right. What matters is that you understand how to use built-in imagery as another tool in your memory tool chest. Here are the "answer" names:

ANSWERS: 1 Bush, 2 Sign, 3 Plank, 4 Taylor, 5 Curtain, 6 Wolfe, 7 Crumb, 8 Water, 9 Shields, 10 Baker

Lessons from Mom: Go to Bed—Now!

You, like everyone else, probably constantly fought with your mother about bedtime. No kid in history has ever gone to bed when his or her mother wanted him to, unless there was an incentive waiting.

But if you can't remember fighting with your mother about bedtime because your memory is so bad, get ready to eat humble pie once again, because she was right. Getting a good night's sleep has been shown to be important in how your brain processes information—including memory.

According to researchers, when you sleep your brain sorts out information that you've been gathering during the time you're awake. A short, thirty-minute nap is ideal for enabling the brain to send recently gathered information to memory networks and organize it into a more usable form (which is why Day 1 included a tip about using sleep to help retain new information, such as cramming for a test—remember?).

A longer sleep period allows the brain to collect, organize, and make sense of information gathered for a longer period of time. For example, if you've just spent the day learning how to ski, after the doctor repairs your broken ankle what you need is a deep sleep cycle that includes REM (rapid eye movement). This type of long, fitful sleep helps your brain sort out all the data gathered about skiing so that you can remember it the next time you hit the slopes. In this respect, REM enables your brain to reevaluate its past experience. This means that all the time your mother was struggling with you so that you'd get a good night's sleep, she was really trying to help your memory.

The Name Is Thomas—Doubting Thomas

At this point, it's likely that there are more than a few Doubting Thomas's out there, shaking your heads. Sure, you say, these memory tools for learning names and faces are fine for meeting a few people at a time. But what about meeting dozens of people, perhaps fifty or more, in a short period of time? How can these memory tools and techniques possibly work in that type of situation? As for an answer to the memory question, there is no doubt that remembering the names of fifty people at one time is a Herculean task. Even someone who can remember whether they had peas or lima beans with their chicken dinner three months ago would have a difficult time with that many names.

The memory tools that you've learned about so far can and do work in that type of situation. It just takes practice, patience, and, above all, confidence. In many respects it's similar to putting together a thousand-piece jigsaw puzzle. When you first open the box and dump the pieces out all over the place, it seems like an impossible task. At this point, you have three options:

1. Put all the pieces back in the box, admit that you made a terrible mistake in ever beginning this, and throw the puzzle away.

2. Hope that tiny elves sneak into your house at night and do the puzzle for you.

3. Break the job up into smaller components: First divide the pieces into distinct groups, such as edge pieces, certain colors, and so on, and then put together a face here and a flower there, until you form mini-pictures that eventually fit together to create a larger picture.

Of course option "3" is the best approach, and it's the same thing with using your memory tools to learn a large number of new names in a short period of time. You have to break up the task into small, manageable sections, and not try to do the entire thing at once. Learn five, or even ten, names, at a time; when you think that you have those committed to memory, go on to the next group. Keep in mind that there is nothing wrong with asking a person to repeat his name, particularly at a large gathering.

Daily Tune-up: Remembering a Group of People at a Party or Business Function

As you know, the best way to keep your car running at peak efficiency is to keep the engine tuned up. Nothing says "I drive a car that should be crushed into a cube" better than a wheezing, sputtering engine with smoke billowing out the tailpipe.

The same thing applies to your memory tools. The best way to keep them sharp and ready for use is to keep them tuned up. The following exercises should help keep your memory tools in tip-top shape:

1. The next time you're at an occasion at which there is a large group of people, such as a family barbecue, practice remembering the names of relatives you don't see often using your memory tools. Even if you know you won't see some of the relatives again until the next family barbecue, use the tools anyway. This will keep them sharp for the next time.

2. The next time you're in a large group of strangers, such as on the subway or train, or at a sporting event, pick out ten people at random. Write down fictitious names for them (based on their facial characteristics, for example), and then try to remember them using your memory tools. If successful, then pick out another group of ten, assign them names, and add them to the list of those you're trying to remember. See how many names you can remember at one time. Give yourself bonus points for using titles (such as Dr., Capt., and Sgt.), coming up with difficult names, or creating outrageous visualizations.

3. Try the same exercise as in number 2, but with magazine or newspaper photographs containing at least six people. Each time you find another ad with at least half a dozen people, add their names to those you're trying to remember.

Practice Drill: Remembering Large Groups

Now here's the tough part of the tune-up, the part where, if this were a car and you were doing an actual tune-up, you would be wedged into some tiny place under the hood. Below is a list of fifty—yes, fifty—names. Using all the memory tools from your tool chest, break the names into groups of ten (the order of the names doesn't matter) and use a separate tool for each one. For instance, use linking for one, visualization for another, and so on. Here are the names:

	Group 1	Group 2	Group 3	Group 4	Group 5
1.	Albright	Farrell	Katzenbach	Paxon	Underwood
2.	Asher	Forsythe	Keating	Popovitch	Upshaw
3.	Besserman	Garcia	Larkin	Quigley	Verde
4.	Brodski	Goldman	Lippincott	Quinlan	Voorhees
5.	Callendar	Henderson	Maldonado	Ramos	Wang
6.	Chang	Holloway	Monroe	Rossi	West
7.	DeLorenzo	Ingram	Nesson	Sansone	Willis
8.	Dressler	Irvin	Nussman	Snyder	Yamamoto
9.	Edwards	Jamal	Oliver	Tetz	Youssef
10.	Erickson	Juliano	Ottinger	Tong	Zahn

I'll help you get started by doing one name from each group.

1. Use linking for group one. For example, the name "Dressler" could become "Dress her."

2. Use linking and imagery for group two. For example, for the name "Goldman" think of a large man, made of gold.

3. Use visualization for group three. For example, for the out-of-the-ordinary name "Katzenbach," first break the name into syllables according to its pronunciation (Cats-in-back), then conjure up an outrageous visualization. Every time you see Mrs. Katzenbach, think of a bevy of felines crawling all around her back, peeking over her shoulders, and poking their heads underneath her elbows.

4. Use imagery with titles for group four. For example, "Sansone" could become Judge Sansone with large glasses who is draping those glasses and wearing a long black judicial robe, or maybe have numerous gavels poking out of those glasses.

5. Use facial features for group five. For example, Mr. Underwood has large ears, so visualize piles and piles of logs stacked up underneath those ears ("under-wood").

Now it's your turn. Good luck.

Tip of the Day

What can you do to help improve your memory beyond the use of mnemonic tools? Choose one of the following below:

A. Tape a list of things you have to remember on your re-frigerator every day.

B. Hire an assistant so that he or she can constantly re-mind you of what you have to remember.

C. Cut down or eliminate the use of caffeine and tobacco.

If you chose "C," then you are correct. Both caffeine and tobacco have been found to adversely impact the brain's memory function.

Researchers in one study have found that smokers record lower performances in short-term memory on verbal tests. Results from another test revealed that both visual and verbal memory was impaired in subjects that smoked more than one pack of cigarettes per day. The findings seem to indicate that smoking interferes with the brain's ability to process information.

As for caffeine, it produces agitation when used excessively.

Since memory works best when the brain is relaxed and alert, the artificially induced state of anxiety caused by caffeine hinders memory.

In Day 4, you will learn how to organize your memory so that it resembles a neat and orderly file cabinet, and not the inside of a china shop after an angry bull visited it.

Day 4

Organizing Your Memory

Like everything else in life, your memory works better if it's organized. Just as it's easier to make a cake if you can quickly find the right ingredients, rather than spending an hour hunting for the flour, it's also easier to remember things that are important if your mind doesn't have to search for the necessary information amid a bunch of random clutter.

Some people, of course, are born organizers; they're the ones who can bring order out of chaos in your sock drawer in a matter of minutes. Others, however, are so disorganized that even finding two matching socks to wear in the morning is a triumph. To find out if you're organized or disorganized, take the following test:

1. Do you regularly get hit with late fees on your credit cards because you took so long to find the time to write out checks or you don't even find your bills until you clean out your purse, which you only do every three months or so?

2. If you get pulled over for speeding, does it take you twenty minutes to go through your glove compartment

to find your registration amid gobs of paper, tapes, pens, and candy wrappers?

3. When you do your taxes, does it take you longer to locate your receipts than it does to actually fill out the tax form?

4. If you're asked to develop an organization chart at work, do you have to first ask someone what that means?

5. If someone bought you an electronic organizer, would you burst out laughing?

If you answered yes to any three of these questions, then you qualify as a bona fide disorganized person. While the mnemonic tools in this chapter will unfortunately not help you balance your checkbook or do your taxes, they will help you organize your memory—and at least that's a start.

Anatomy 101: Using Your Body to Remember Items

What do you see when you open a file cabinet? Almost inevitably, inside you find numerous folders, each containing papers and other documents about a specific subject. When you organize your memory, you are trying to keep basic information grouped according to subject—trying to keep memories in specific folders, so to speak.

Of course, in order to do this you have to create mental file folders to store information. One way to do this is to create the folders out of something that is already part of your long-term memory, and which you can't forget. This ensures that they will always be there when you need them. For example, as bad as your memory is, you can't forget the days of the week. At some point in your life the name of each day entered your long-term memory, and there they remain. Every once in a while you might have trouble *recalling* which day of the week it is, but that isn't a problem with long-term memory as much as it is a temporary condition brought about by stress or other factors. You can always recite the days of the week.

Something else that you can easily remember is the parts of your body. No matter how bad your memory is, if you can't remember where your toes are, or which is your elbow and which is your hand, then you've got something more serious going on than just a poor memory. Since you can easily remember the parts of your body, you can use them to help organize your memory.

Exercise: Body Numbering

The first step in the process of creating mental file folders from parts of your body is to give each body part a number. Starting from either the head or feet, assign each body part a number, beginning with number one. Then work either upward or downward, depending upon where you started. Remember, there really is no *wrong* way to do this, as long as whichever way you choose works for you, and you remain consistent and the numbered parts follow a logical progression.

Here's a simple exercise. Start numbering your body parts with the top of your body—the head. Now, number the following body parts from one to ten: head, face, shoulders, elbows, hands, stomach, thighs, knees, feet, and toes. Now, repeat this exercise a few times until you're confident that you have both body parts and their respective numbers fixed in your mind. It may help if, while you are repeating this, you touched each body part to further strengthen the association.

How did it go? What you're doing with this numeric technique is creating mental file folders to store information. Another way to think of these folders is as memory pegs, onto which information can be hung for easy retrieval. We'll talk more about pegs in a subsequent chapter.

Now That I Have This List, What Do I Do with It?

Good question. What you're going to do now is something similar to the linking techniques that you learned earlier in the book. However, the difference is that before, you were linking two or more new items together. Here, using these memory folders or pegs that you've created from body parts, you're going to be linking new information with known information.

For example, let's say there are ten things you want to look for at the department store. Although you've made a list of these items, you forgot to bring it. Here's where your body parts list/mental file folders come in handy.

Say that the first item you want to see is curtains. Place this item into one of your mental file folders by pegging it to body part number one—the head. You might do this by imagining that there is a curtain rod balanced on top of your head, with curtains hanging down on both sides.

However, while this is a good start, it isn't enough. Remember you previously learned that one of the important aspects of any visual image you create is to make it humorous and exaggerated. While it may seem like curtains hanging down on both sides of your head is a funny image, it might also be easily forgotten because it isn't striking enough. To make the image more outrageous—and therefore, unforgettable—how about giving the curtains a wild design, such as huge, psychedelic pink flowers?

Still, you can go further. Instead of having those bizarre flowers just lying quietly on the curtains, how about making them rotate? What about having giant bumblebees buzzing in and out of them? Or what about having those pink flowers as part of a large garden that's alive with activity—bees buzzing, butterflies flitting about, ants and caterpillars walking on plant stems, and other flowers waving in the breeze? Remember, the more vivid and lively you can make the image, the more likely it is that you won't forget. You should be able to smell the flowers, hear the bees buzzing, and feel the breeze on your face.

Now, when you think about the first item on your list, is it easier to remember plain white curtains hanging down on both sides of your head, or curtains with giant pink flowers surrounded by a virtual hive of plant and insect activity? If you've made the image memorable enough, when you want to remember what the first item is on your list, you should be able to just dig into mental file folder number one and find curtains.

Congratulations! You've now put—or pegged—into mental file folders an item that you need to remember to buy at the department store. If you do the same with the rest of the items, putting one item into each file folder and creating an outrageous visualization to go with it, you can easily remember each and every item. Just open each mental file folder when you get to the store, and there the items are: curtains, light bulbs, and so on. This is how you organize your memory.

Exercise: Running Errands

Now that you've learned how to organize your memory via mental file folders, test your new knowledge with the following exercise. Below is a list of ten errands along with a mental file folder for each task. Organize your memory by placing each errand into a file folder, creating a visualization for each.

Now here's a catch. The tasks can be done in any order, but, just to make things a bit more challenging, the file folders are not arranged in an organized manner. You're going to have to organize them as well.

Task	File Folder
1. Buying stamps	Shoulders
2. Picking up dry cleaning	Head
3. Returning videos	Toes
4. Getting gas	Stomach
5. Returning an item to a store	Thighs
6. Going to the library	Elbows
7. Getting a watch repaired at the jeweler's	Face
8. Buying bagels	Knees
9. Bringing the dog to the vet	Feet
10. Dropping off shoes to be repaired	Hands

How did you do? Did you make the images vivid, outrageous, and funny? Are you smiling now as you think about them? If you are, then you've done your job well. And, while you've heard me say that there are no right answers to many of these exercises as long as the image is memorable to you, here is the most logical order for organizing your mental file folders: head, face, shoulders, elbows, hands, stomach, thighs, knees, feet, and toes.

Quiz: Remembering What You Just Did

Here's a quiz to see if you really did make your mental images as vivid and outrageous as possible. Think of your list of file folders. Then, without looking at the list above, and moving in an organized fashion from top to bottom, remember which errand you put into each folder.

Can you remember them all? If you cannot, then the images for some are probably not vivid enough. Go back and work on those images until they're fixed in your mind. This is a way to get into the habit of remembering things by pegging them in file folders, until you've gotten the hang of creating your visualizations.

Remember, make your visualizations for your mental file folders as "wild and crazy" as possible. Exaggerate and animate the images, and make up weird and unusual situations that would never happen in real life. Imagine that you're a cartoon artist, and you're trying to create outlandish images and situations that make you laugh. Not only will this help your memory, but it will also make the entire task fun and thus more appealing.

Don't Stop There

This method of organizing your memory into mental file folders depends upon using information stored into your long-term memory and which you can't forget. For example, you can't possibly forget where your feet are—even if you try! Thus, when you create mental file folders out of parts of your body, you always know where your feet are, for example, and you will always be able to use them as a file folder.

But why stop there? Why stop with just creating mental file folders out of body parts? After all, there are almost certainly many other things in your life that you can use as mental file folders.

For instance, what about the rooms in your house (or as I mentioned earlier, the days of the week)? Surely, if you close your eyes right now and picture your living room in your mind, you see exactly how it is laid out—where the chairs, the couch, and television are, and so on. If you chose a number of items from the living room, they could also function as mental file folders. Again, you use the images to create mental file folders logically. Remember, when you devise your visualization, make it humorous, exaggerated, and fun, with plenty of action. However, as long as you follow the same procedure that you used to create your body parts file folders, there is no reason why other things won't work just as well.

Exercise: Practice Using Mental File Folders

For this exercise use the room file folders mentioned above. Let's say that you've created a set of six new file folders, based on the way your living room is organized, as follows:

1. Sofa

2. Television

3. Fireplace

4. Lamp

5. Easy chair

6. Grandfather clock

Now, let's say you need to put six items you have to remember at the grocery store into these folders. The items are: bacon, eggs, bread, milk, chicken, and apples. Place these items into the living room file folders you've just created, and come up with a visualization for each one.

All done? Good. Compare how you did with the examples below.

1. **Sofa—bacon.** Picture pigs on your sofa, watching television with their hooves on the coffee table while they gobble up bags of chips and gallons of soda.

2. **Television—eggs.** On your television are eggs, not just
   a couple, but dozens and dozens. The heat from the TV
   is making them burst open like bombs, sending showers
   of sticky yellow yolk all over the room.

3. **Fireplace—bread.** There are numerous bakers
   swarming around your fireplace, making bread,
   reaching into the fireplace with long wooden paddles to
   take out more golden brown loaves. Because there are so
   many bakers, they keep bumping into each other and
   falling down.

4. **Lamp—milk.** The lamp shade is made not of fabric,
   but glass milk bottles that keep clicking and clacking
   into each other as if they're being buffeted by a strong
   wind.

5. **Easy chair—chicken.** There are chickens scrambling
   about everywhere on your easy chair, running up and
   down the back and sides, pecking at the pillows, and
   squawking so loudly that you can't hear the TV. To
   make matters worse, the air is choked with feathers.

6. **Grandfather clock—apples.** The numbers on the face
   of the clock are covered in red, green, and yellow apples.
   You can see the apples moving each time the second
   hand moves around the clock.

Were you able to devise visualizations as vivid and exaggerated as those above? Did you remember to put the grocery items into the file folders in a logical order? If you forgot either the file folders or could not devise a visualization, repeat the exercise again until you become more confident and familiar with the idea of creating mental file folders.

Open the Memory Tool Chest: Substitution

Do you remember how, when you were in school, the knowledge that you were going to have a substitute instead of your regular teacher sent you into fits of euphoria? That's because you knew that having a substitute meant it was going to be an easy day; no substitute would risk messing up the regular teacher's normal routine.

For those of you who like the idea that some things never change, using the substitution tool from your memory tool chest also means that you're going to have it easy—but in this case, it's ease of remembering. Using substitute words and/or phrases helps you easily remember abstract words, names, and concepts that might prove difficult to commit to memory otherwise.

How does the substitution tool work? Like all good tools, easily and effectively. Essentially, what you are doing when you use this tool is breaking up an abstract word or phrase into something far more common and easy to recall.

For instance, let's say it's imperative you remember that your new boss came from the Cincinnati branch office. All alone, Cincinnati might prove difficult to commit to memory. But how about "sin-sin-at-tea?" Your visualization is two old-time preachers in long black frock coats sitting at a small table drinking tea. Picture the preachers' bony arms and legs, their thin fingers as they pour the tea, and the way their wire-rimmed glasses sit ever so delicately on their noses.

This, essentially, is how your substitution memory tool works. It can be used whenever you need to remember an abstract word, name, or concept. For example, say that you want to remember to sign up for a postgraduate course in American History—but you know that you'll forget to do that in the crush of everything else that you have to do once you arrive on campus.

But while you may not remember "American History," you'll probably remember "A-merry-can His-story," particularly if your visualization is vivid and humorous, such as a laughing watering can telling "his" story. Can't you see the big smile on the happy can's face, with the spout serving as his nose and one eye on either side of the spout, as he stands on a soapbox like an orator, telling his humorous story to various people walking by?

You've now added another powerful memory tool to your tool chest: substitution. The key, as it is with other memory tools, is to have fun with the visualization and make it vivid and witty. Also, don't worry about the spelling of your substitute phrase either; this is no place for English teachers. You're trying to come up with substitute words and phrases to help your memory, not win the National Grammar Award.

Tool Time, Part 1: What City, Please?

Now that you know how to use your latest memory tool, try this exercise to hone your abilities. For example, you're a newly hired salesman for a pharmaceutical company and you have to travel to the following six American cities to meet with clients. Develop substitute words and/or phrases, and then visualizations, for the following destinations:

1. Indianapolis

2. Phoenix

3. Dover

4. Richmond

5. Cleveland

6. Seattle

Time's up! How did you do? Here are some suggested sub-stitute words and phrases and visualization:

1. **Indian-at-poles:** An Indian standing next to a pole of some type (telephone, barber, and so on).

2. **Fee-nix:** A gigantic word "Fee" emphatically shaking its head no (as in "nix").

3. **Doe-fur:** A forest full of female deer with luscious brown fur.

4. **Rich-man:** A very wealthy man dressed like a billionaire (like the Monopoly character), holding a bag of money.

5. **Cleave-land:** A huge cleaver, such as in a slasher movie, cutting in two a large piece of land, such as the North American continent.

6. **See-At-tell:** A person named "At" telling all that he knows about a bank robbery to a policeman, while you watch.

Tool Time, Part 2: Son of Substitution

Just as all the best movies have sequels, here's another chance to practice using the substitution memory tool.

Below are ten random phrases, things, and concepts, along with a reason why you may need to remember them. Using your substitution tool, devise a substitute word or phrase and a visualization for each boldfaced word.

1. **Maryland:** Your old college roommate lives in Maryland.

2. **Bacteria:** You are preparing for a final exam or test or a continuing education class in biology and you have to remember the different types of infections.

3. **Roman Empire:** You are helping your child with a project for history class.

4. **Champagne:** You are taking a wine-tasting class.

5. **Utah:** You are doing your genealogy and have to know where your great-grandparents were born.

6. **Lincoln:** You are a research assistant gathering archive photos of leaders during war.

7. **Hammock:** You are doing your Christmas shopping and need to remember to buy your sister and brother-in-law a present.

8. **Destiny:** It's your best friend's birthday and you need to recall the name of her favorite perfume to buy for her.

9. **Edison:** You are visiting your cousin in New Jersey and need to remember that Edison is the third stop on the train line.

10. **Salmon:** Your niece is coming to visit for two weeks and she loves seafood, but is allergic to salmon.

Pencils down. How did you do this time? See if your answers are similar to the suggestions below.

1. Maryland
   Substitution: "Mary's-land"
   Visualization: Picture a hillside covered with baby girls named Mary. Perhaps they can be wearing little shirts that say "Mary" on them, or maybe they resemble a Mary that you know.

2. Bacteria
   Substitution: "Back-tear."
   Visualization: Think of a very nice coat, sweater, or shirt that has a jagged, full-length tear straight down the back.

3. Roman Empire

   Substitution: "Roaming-umpire."

   Visualization: Think of a baseball umpire roaming the field, holding his mask in his hands as he wanders about as if he doesn't have a clue.

4. Champagne

   Substitution: "Champ-pain."

   Visualization: Think of a boxing champion in the ring, fighting a tough opponent, and wincing as he takes a thunderous blow to the rib cage.

5. Utah

   Substitution: "You-tear."

   Visualization: Picture yourself ripping up stacks and stacks of papers—bills, mortgages, legal notices, whatever makes the image more memorable for you.

6. Lincoln

   Substitution: "Link-one."

   Visualization: Picture yourself linking things together, one after another, until you've got a trail that goes on for miles and miles, such as sausage links, blocks, lengths of chain, or whatever else you can think of.

7. Hammock

   Substitution: "Ham-mock."

   Visualization: Picture a sarcastic pig ridiculing everything that anyone does. Maybe he's on stage in a Las Vegas nightclub, microphone in hand.

8. Destiny

   Substitution: "Dust-tiny."

   Visualization: An effective visualization is a bunch of tiny house cleaners, scrambling all over each other to dust pieces of furniture in a home.

9. Edison
    Substitution: "Ed's-son."
    Visualization: Picture an "Ed"—any Ed, even Mr.
    Ed, the famous talking horse—and then picture his son
    with him. If you don't know any Eds make one up.
    Dress him in an outlandish costume, and put the same
    type of clothes on his son as well.

10. Salmon
    Substitution: "Sam-one."
    Visualization: Sounds like something that pilots in
    military aircraft would say to each other, doesn't it? Try
    visualizing the pilots in their flight uniforms, the sun
    gleaming off their sunglasses as they say into the
    microphone in their hand: "Sam-one, Sam-one, can
    you read me?"

Lessons from Mom: Fish as Brain Food

"Eat your fish. It's brain food."

Can't you just hear your mother saying that even now,
from years ago when you used to sit at the dinner table in
your house, miserably pushing a piece of fish around on your
plate with a fork and hoping it would disappear? But that was
just an old saying, wasn't it? Fish isn't really brain food, is it?

Now don't faint as you sit there today eating your fast food
hamburger or slice of pizza, but your mother was right again.
A growing body of scientific evidence is pointing to the fact
that fish is, indeed, brain food.

According to the latest scientific research, most fish fat
contains the polyunsaturated fatty acid DHA, which plays a
major role in the development of the brain and central nervous system in young children. Studies have revealed that

children who receive a sufficient amount of DHA perform better on intelligence tests than those without an adequate dietary intake of DHA.

Because of these findings, infant formula makers have been seeking ways to add DHA to their products. Ironically, one of the best sources of DHA is cod liver oil—a substance almost as universally despised among kids as fish! Fish as brain food? It's true. And, of course, whatever helps your brain helps your memory. Sorry to ruin your lunch—but you should have known by now that you couldn't beat Mom.

Daily Tune-up: Acrostics and Acronyms

Just as a car runs best when it's tuned up, so do your memory tools work best when you take them out of your memory toolbox on occasion and use them, even if the situation doesn't require it.

In Day 1, you learned about acronyms (making a word out of the first letters of the words to be remembered) and acrostics (the first letters in a series of words, lines, or verses form the information to be remembered). Below are more examples of acronyms and acrostics. After you refresh your memory, keep both of those memory tools sharp by coming up with any combination of five more acrostics and/or acronyms.

Acronyms

- **SPA:** A chronological listing of famous philosophers: Socrates taught Plato who taught Aristotle.
- **Roy G. Biv:** The colors of the spectrum: red, orange, yellow, green, blue, indigo, violet.

- **NATO:** North Atlantic Treaty Organization.
- **LASER:** Light Amplification by Stimulated Emission of Radiation.
- **DARE:** Drug and Alcohol Resistance Education.
- **MADD:** Mothers Against Drunk Driving.
- **NASA:** National Aeronautics and Space Administration.
- **NAFTA:** North America Free Trade Agreement
- **RADAR:** Radio Detection and Ranging.

Acrostics

- **Please Excuse My Dear Aunt Sally:** How to solve an algebraic equation: Parentheses, Exponents, Multiplication, Division, Addition, Subtraction.

- **All Cows Eat Grass:** The spaces on a bass note staff: A, C, E, and G.

- **Good Boys Do Fine Always:** The lines on a treble note scale: G, B, D, F, and A.

Tip of the Day

Don't you just hate it when you have this great dream that you remember when you first wake up, only to completely forget it a few minutes later?

It doesn't matter if your dream involves winning an Olympic medal or a million dollars—it's often both interesting and informative to remember your dreams. Writers and artists have been influenced by their dreams; supposedly, Mary Wollstonecraft Shelley based her classic novel *Frankenstein* on fragments of a dream.

In order to remember your dreams, you really have to want to remember them. This is because it requires you to change your sleeping habits. If, like the post office, neither rain, snow, sleet, or hail can keep you from your appointed time in dreamland, then you're going to have to be satisfied with fuzzy memories.

But if you want to remember in what event you won the Olympic medal, here's what to do: Before falling asleep, repeatedly tell yourself, "I want to wake up at the end of my dream so I can write it down." After a few attempts, you should be able to plant this autosuggestion firmly in your mind. Make sure you have paper, pencil, and a flashlight handy so that you can write down all the necessary details of your dream once you wake up. You never know which one holds the key to interpreting the dream.

If you don't dream today like you used to when you were in college, don't worry; studies have shown that as you age, you dream less often than younger people, possibly because of a decline in spontaneous mental imagery related to aging. However, research also seems to indicate that the ability to form mental images is a skill that can be relearned, no matter what the age.

In Day 5, you'll learn how to use your newly acquired memory skills to remember everyday tasks.

Day 5

Using Your Memory Skills for Everyday Tasks, Part I

A day doesn't go by that you don't have to remember or recite a number. It doesn't matter if it's a telephone number, credit card number, or personal identification number, numbers play a crucial role in your professional and personal life.

Remembering Numbers

Face it, remembering numbers has become a prerequisite for living in the modern age. Although many people worry that the growing use of numbers is increasing the depersonalization of our society, it is a fact that each technological breakthrough seems to bring yet another number or set of numbers for us to remember in order just to be able to function. Social Security numbers, telephone-fax-cellular numbers, five- (and now nine-!) digit Zip Codes, credit card PINs, home security system codes, computer passwords—the list is endless.

Numbers are difficult to remember because they are abstract, unlike a name, which you can usually relate to something. For instance, if the model of your computer printer was the Big Horizon Blue, you'd probably remember it because it has a distinctive name. If you couldn't, then some of the mnemonic tools discussed such as linking and visualization could help you remember the name. But if your printer model is the SuperJet 44056, it becomes more difficult to remember, particularly because the entire line of SuperJet printers all use similar numbers, such as 44054, 44057, and 44058.

Sometimes, you use a number so often that despite its length or complexity it becomes part of your long-term memory. If your telephone banking system asks you for your Social Security number every time you use it, then it's likely that you'll quickly memorize it. By the same token, not many of you have your driver's license number memorized, because that information is seldom required.

It's almost certain that a day doesn't go by that you aren't faced with the need to either remember or utilize a number. For that reason, you're going to start to look at how you can use your memory skills to help you in performing everyday tasks by examining memory tools to help you remember numbers.

Visualization

Dig around in your memory tool chest until you find one of its most useful tools—visualization. Hard as it is to believe, visualization can help you to remember numbers.

Suppose you have to remember the number 648. By itself, there is nothing very distinctive about that number. However, what if you visualize it painted in large, Day-Glo colors on a solid white wall? Or what if the numbers formed fiery red coals that glowed fiercely everywhere you looked? No matter where you were, you saw that number sizzling out at you, whether it was on the back of a co-worker's shirt or on the dashboard of your car. Just as before, the key to making the visualization tool work effectively is the vividness of the visualization. To further reinforce the image, try devising a verbal statement about the number. For instance, for 648 you could make up a rhyme: "6-4-8, who do you appreciate? Me!"

Turning Numbers into Words

Another effective method for remembering numbers is to turn them into words. One of the most common ways to do this is to give each number 1 through 9 its letter equivalent: A=1, B=2, C=3, and so on. Using this system, the number 852 (with three digits, 8-5-2) would become HEB. Of course, by itself HEB means nothing, so you have to turn it into an acronym or acrostic that you can remember, such as "Hairy Elephant Backs" (that's an acrostic). Now, when you have to remember the number 852, just say the phrase "Hairy Elephant Backs" and turn the first letters of each word back into their appropriate numbers.

Exercise: Remembering Work-Related Numbers

In your professional life you may be asked to remember quantities of various items for events or presentations. For example, if you are an office manager or administrative assistant you may be responsible for keeping track of important numbers such as phone extensions, quarterly budget totals, and office supplies. Using the memory tool of turning numbers into words (acrostics), memorize the following five numbers for office tasks.

1. 46 is the number of lunches you order for the monthly managers meeting.

2. 35 is the number of packages of paper you order monthly for the photocopier.

3. 357 is the extension of the technical department.

4. 215 is the password for the security system.

5. 36 is the number of employees that work in your department.

Were you able to devise words for each of the numbers? Here are some suggestions:

1. The number 46 becomes DF. When you need to order lunch for the next meeting think of the acrostic "Deli Food."

2. The number 35 becomes CE. The next time you are filling out the order form for supplies think of the acrostic "Copier Empty" to remember how many packages of copier paper you need.

3. The number 357 becomes CEG. Every week when you call the technical department for updates on the computer programs think of the acrostic "Computer Equipment Glitches."

4. The number 215 becomes BAE. The next time you enter the security system remember the acrostic "Burglar Alarm End."

5. The number 36 becomes CF. Every time you have to print out memos or company-related materials for your department think of the acrostic "Computer Forms" to remember how many people work in your department.

Pop Quiz: Making Numbers Memorable

Using the two memory tools just discussed—visualization and turning numbers into words—try to memorize the following ten numbers. Use visualization for numbers one through five and turn numbers six through ten into words.

1. 845

2. 921

3. 148

4. 632

5. 1,643

6. 498

7. 374

8. 1,759

9. 1,472

10. 16,790

How did you do? I'll give you a hand. For example, for the number 845, picture a telephone keypad with the numbers 845 flashing in different colors. And the number 498 would become DIH. You could turn it into an acrostic such as "Dogs In House."

The Picture Code

A memory tool that is more advanced is a visual peg system called a picture code (Remember I promised in Day 4 that I would talk about pegs?). In this method, you assign each number a symbol, based on its appearance. As you look at the numbers and their corresponding symbols below, use your imagination to see how they go together:

0 = plate

1 = spear

2 = swan

3 = pitchfork

4 = sailboat

5 = spread-out hand

6 = snake

7 = gallows

8 = hourglass

9 = snail

Next, memorize each of these symbols and their corresponding number. After you've done that, you are ready to use the method. For example, to remember your flight number, let's say it's 427, picture a sailboat with a swan on board that is sailing by a gallows.

Exercise: Code Deciphering

Use the picture code tool to devise pictures or images for the following numbers:

1. 638

2. 726

3. 194

4. 3,760

5. 5,839

How did you do? Below are some suggested pictures. If you had trouble remembering any of the symbols for each number, keep working at them until you're confident that you know them.

1. 638—A snake with a pitchfork sticking through its body climbing up an hourglass.

2. 726—A gallows with a swan swinging in its noose, while a snake crawls along its top beam.

3. 194—A spear sticking through a snail that is lying on a sailboat.

4. 3,760—A pitchfork sticking through a gallows, on top of which a snake is lying on a plate.

5. 5,839—A spread-out hand on top of an hourglass, with a pitchfork that has a snail atop one of its prongs.

The Phonetic Number Code System

Perhaps the most complex memory tool that you can use to remember numbers is the Phonetic Number Code System. Although it is complicated, if you can master it, then you will be able to remember long strings of numbers. For that reason it is very useful and worth the effort to learn how to use.

In this method, each number is assigned a consonant or consonant sound based upon the following visualizations:

0 = z, s (0 is zero)

1 = t (a "t" looks like a 1 with a line through it)

2 = n ("n" has two bars, just like a 2)

3 = m ("m" has three bars, just like a 3)

4 = r ("r" is the last letter in the word "four")

5 = l (in Roman numerals, "l" is the sign for 50)

6 = soft g or j sound and also ch and sh (6 resembles a capital "G")

7 = k (a "k" looks like a vertical bar)

8 = f, v (an "f" written in script has two loops, just like an 8)

9 = p, b (a 9 looks like a "p" reversed or an upside-down "b")

Now, here's how you apply the Phonetic Number Code System. Take the number's corresponding consonant sound or sounds, and then add vowels to make either a short group of words or even a sentence. For example, the telephone number 641-8950 becomes the following: grt-fbls. By adding vowels, you can come up with the following phrase: "great fables."

As you can see right away, the one flaw in this method is that all the consonants and consonant sounds must be perfectly memorized in order for it to work. However, once you have accomplished this, there is no limit to how much you can use this memory tool, or how long you can retain the information. For instance, while the telephone number 641-8950 is not easy to remember, the phrase "great fables" is. Every time you need to remember that particular telephone number, the phrase "great fables" should pop right into your mind.

Exercise: Turning Something Out of Nothing

Below are five everyday uses of numbers. Use the Phonetic Number Code System to turn the corresponding numbers into groups of words, or even a short sentence.

1. Lock combination for athletic club locker: 3-41-10

2. Social Security number: 135-37-0994

3. ATM identification number: 90501

4. Zip Code: 50368

5. Telephone number: 801-9476

How did you do? Most likely you found it difficult, at least initially. However, like any tool, the longer you use it, the more familiar with it you'll become. The key is not to give up in frustration; take your time, keep trying, and eventually you'll find yourself just as proficient with this memory tool as you've become with all the others.

Just in case you couldn't translate some of the numbers, here are some suggestions:

1. 3-41-10 becomes m-rt-ts, which can be translated into "more right turns."

2. 135-37-0994 becomes tml-mk-sppr, which can be translated into "tamales make supper."

3. 90501 becomes ps-lst, which can be translated into "pass list."

4. 50368 becomes lsmgf, which can be translated into "light smog fumes."

5. 801-9476 becomes fst-brkg, which can be translated into "fast breaking."

Memory Sharpener: How to Remember Foreign Language Phrases

In today's global economy, when anyone you want to reach anywhere in the world is at the end of your telephone or computer line, it's often important to know some foreign words or phrases. Unfortunately, just like numbers, remembering random phrases in an unfamiliar language is very difficult, because you cannot relate them to anything.

In a moment I'll discuss a memory tool that you can use to

help you remember foreign words and phrases. First, however, here's a list of general guidelines that should help make learning a foreign language easier:

1. In order to learn another language, practice both passive understanding, such as reading (recognition), and active usage, such as in writing and speaking (recall).

2. Continually expose yourself to the language in written and oral form. Otherwise, while your passive understanding remains, your active use of the language withers from neglect. Therefore, try listening to radio station broadcasts in the language you're learning, or listening to language tapes or audio books. Going to see a movie in the language, or reading a book that is written in the language, helps maintain your active use.

3. Above all, speak the language whenever you can—at home, to a neighbor or friend, or even take a foreign language class. Like anything else, the more you use it, the less likely you are to lose it.

Tool Time: A Two-Step Technique to Help You Remember Foreign Words and Phrases

Here is yet another example of how visualization plays a key role in sharpening your memory: Using visualization is part of the two-step memory technique to help you remember foreign words and phrases.

For example, the French word for bridge is *pont*. To remember this word, change it into a similar English word, such as *punt*. Now here's where visualization comes into play: Imagine yourself punting a bridge in a football game. To make the image memorable, imagine yourself punting the bridge downfield to opposing players, who are looking up in shock at what they expected to be a football but have suddenly realized is a bridge.

One more. The Spanish word for water is *agua,* which is similar to an English word for water, *aqua.* Your visualization is, simply, water—a great shimmering pool of cool, crystal clear water you are swimming in.

Exercise: When in France

Below are four French words and their English equivalents. Using the two-step technique, change each word into English, and devise a visualization for each example.

1. Pluie (rain)
2. Chien (dog)
3. Neige (snow)
4. Une Glace (ice cream)

How did you do? Are you ready to hop on a plane, head for France, and roam the streets of Paris as a Bohemian artist, speaking fluent French? Below are some suggestions.

1. Pluie (rain)
   English word: Plenty.
   Visualization: Plenty of rain pouring down, drenching you as you walk.
2. Chien (dog)
   English word: Chain.
   Visualization: A big, ferocious dog on a chain, straining and fighting to break free.
3. Neige (snow)
   English word: Neglect.

Visualization: Think of yourself neglecting to shovel a foot of snow that's waiting for you outside.

4. Une Glace (ice cream)
   English word: A glance.
   Visualization: Think of yourself hungrily glancing at a delicious ice cream cone that contains your favorite flavor.

The Dreaded Public Speaking Beast

Ask a hundred guests at a party what they fear most and it's almost certain that at least half of them will say "public speaking."

Indeed, many people dread being asked to speak in public. The most erudite, self-assured businessperson can become sweaty-palmed and nervous at the mere thought of having to address a group of people.

Here are a few memory-related strategies to help you face the dreaded public speaking beast:

- Don't memorize your speech word for word—it will only come out sounding as stale as month-old bread. Also there's the danger of forgetting parts of your speech, and then not knowing what to say at all.

- Don't read it word for word. Your speech will bore your audience and not help them focus on your message.

- Use the loci memory tool (discussion below) to help you deliver your speech in a clear, straightforward manner, as if you're having a casual conversation with the audience. What's the memory tool of loci, you ask? Good question.

The Loci Method

Loci is probably the oldest mnemonic tool. The word is the plural of "locus," which means "place or direction." This method was supposedly developed back in 500 B.C., when a poet who survived a building collapse was able to identify the victims by where they were sitting. Subsequently, both Greek and Roman orators used the loci method to speak without notes. They would simply imagine objects that represented the topics they wanted to talk about, and then mentally place those objects in various locations throughout the building or room where they were speaking. Each time the speaker reached a different location, he mentally retrieved his object or topic from it.

Loci is a very powerful and useful addition to your memory tool chest if you use it correctly. The most important thing to remember when using loci is to choose a location that you know well, such as your home or office. Don't choose a place you've only visited once, such as a park; the location has to automatically spring to mind, and be embedded in your long-term memory.

Loci and Public Speaking: How It Works

This is a technique you are already familiar with from Day 4—it's similar to the mental file folders you created from your body parts or furniture in a room. Here is how you can apply this method to public speaking. To use loci to remember a speech, first choose your location; for the sake of this discussion, let's pick your home. As with other memory tools, loci works only when it's used in a logical, predictable sequence. Start by entering the front door of your home, then go into the living room, the dining room, and so on, continuing through the house in a logical fashion. Next, place the main point of your speech in the first location—in this case, the front door. Then you mentally move around your home, placing the second and third points and so on to their corresponding locations in your home. When you're ready to speak, visualize yourself going into your home, retrieving the first point of your speech from the front door, and starting your speech.

For example, the first point you want to make is to welcome the audience members who have come from the company's Colorado branch office. On the front door of your home you place a big "Welcome" sign, perhaps draped over the jagged cliffs of the Rocky Mountains. Your second point is a summary of your division's activities for the fourth quarter. The next thing you see in your home is the television, so place four quarters on top of the TV (for "fourth quarter"), along with the word "summary." (You could also think of watching the fourth quarter of a televised football game on the TV screen.)

Each time you come to another location in your home, retrieve the next point in your speech. By using this method, you can deliver a speech that is professional, yet comes across as natural to your audience.

Giving a Speech: New Kid in Town

At some point, almost everyone in a managerial role has to make a speech introducing a new employee to the other members of his or her department. Although on the surface it seems a simple task, in reality you, as the manager, are not only trying to ease the way for your new employee but are also making a lasting impression on this new person. If you stumble, stammer, and forget most of your new worker's credentials, the impression you'll make will undoubtedly be a negative one.

You can make written notes, but why bother when your memory tools are just perfect for an occasion like this? Use the mental file folders that you created using your body parts. Let's see how this works with an example: Susan Dell.

Practice Drill: Introducing Susan Dell

Below on the left are eight points you want to emphasize about Susan Dell, your new employee. On the right are your body parts mental file folders ("head" is number 1). Organize both lists so that each point goes into the correct file folder, according to the order in which you want to speak about each point. Then, devise a humorous or exaggerated visualization for each so that each point sticks firmly in your memory.

Points	*Folders*
1. Comes from Wilmington office	Hands
2. Has been with company twelve years	Thighs
3. Has MBA in marketing	Arms
4. Previously worked on company's sunblock product line	Knees
5. Developed slogan "Sunburn Is for Amateurs"	Face
6. Will oversee new anti-aging cream product line	Stomach
7. Has three children	Head
8. Enjoys baseball	Shoulders

How did you do? As for the visualizations, remember that there is no wrong answer; whatever works best for you is correct. However, here are some suggestions just in case you got stuck:

1. **Head:** Comes from Wilmington office
   Visualization: The Wilmington office balanced precariously on your head.

2. **Face:** Has been with company twelve years
   Visualization: A large number 12 painted on your face.

3. **Shoulders:** Has MBA in marketing
   Visualization: Giant fire engine red letters spelling out "MBA" rising up on both shoulders like mountains.

4. **Arms:** Previously worked on company's sunblock product line
   Visualization: The sun, in full football gear, blocking other suns in a play taking place on your arms.

5. **Hands:** Developed slogan "Sunburn Is for Amateurs"
   Visualization: An amateur play taking place on your hands by actors who are incredibly sunburned.

6. **Stomach:** Will oversee new anti-aging cream product line
   Visualization: A wrinkled stomach that the new employee is putting cream on.

7. **Thighs:** Has three children
   Visualization: Three children playfully scampering up and down your thighs.

8. **Knees:** Enjoys baseball
   Visualization: A baseball bat balanced on your knee.

Pop Quiz: The Versatile System of Loci

Now that you've learned the basics of loci, explore other ways to use this versatile memory tool. Like the other memory tools that are safely tucked away in your memory tool chest, loci can be used in a variety of ways.

For example, use loci to memorize long lists. Say, for instance, that you have to remember the Seven Deadly Sins: pride, avarice, lust, anger, gluttony, envy, and sloth. Using the loci method, you would place each of the sins on various locations throughout your house, starting with pride on your front door (picture a giant face on your front door looking so smug and proud).

Use your loci memory tool to remember long lists that cover any topic or subject, such as the Ten Commandments or the ten amendments that make up the Bill of Rights to a list of products you need to purchase at the hardware store.

Open the Memory Tool Chest: Using the Link and Substitute Word Tools

Just like loci, your link and substitute word memory tools can be used to help you perform everyday tasks. For example, let's say you want to memorize the fifty states in alphabetical order. This is a perfect job for the link and substitute word tools. For example, in alphabetical order, numbers 12, 13, 14, and 15 are the "I" states: Idaho, Illinois, Indiana, and Iowa. To use the link and substitute word tools, first devise a substitute word or phrase for each state: Ida-hoeing (Idaho), Ill-noise (Illinois), Indian (Indiana), and I-owe-ya (Iowa). Next, link each of these together and visualize the link: see Ida hoeing while an ill noise sounds, while in the background are a group of Indians saying to each other "I owe ya."

Another way to use the substitute words tool is to think of pictures that recall each state for you. In the above example, potatoes represent Iowa, Chicago's Wrigley Field for Illinois, Indianapolis 500 for Indiana, and so on. You could then link these images together, such as having potatoes being delivered to Wrigley Field in Chicago while racing cars zoom around the infield.

No matter how you use the tools, however, remember that, first and foremost, the images must have meaning for you. So if your brother lives in Illinois, then use him as a substitute word/image for the state, and think of potatoes being delivered to him while racing cars zip around his front yard.

Here's another example using link and substitute word tools. For example, say that you are helping your child prepare for a test on remembering the order of the U.S. presidents. Presidents number 11 through number 14 are James Polk, Zachary Taylor, Millard Fillmore, and Franklin Pierce. Substitute words for each one are:

1. Poke (Polk)
2. Tailor (Taylor)
3. Fill-more (Fillmore)
4. Pierce (Pierce)

To link these words together, visualize someone *poking a tailor,* who is trying to *fill more* holes that someone has *pierced* in a shirt.

Exercise: Using the Link and Substitute Word Tools

Now it's your turn. Below are states number 43 through number 46 in alphabetical order; use your substitute word and your link memory tools to help you remember them in order:

43. Texas
44. Utah
45. Vermont
46. Virginia

Let's practice some more. Below are five states along with their capital cities. Again use the link and substitute word tools to remember them:

1. New Jersey—Trenton
2. Maine—Augusta
3. Arizona—Phoenix
4. Mississippi—Jackson
5. Nevada—Carson City

Lessons from Mom: Take Your Vitamins!

Do you remember how your mother always told you (and may still tell you) to take your vitamins? Usually that meant swallowing some multivitamin pill. Being kids, of course, you always gave your mom a hard time or didn't swallow the pill. Of course, if Mom dared to serve healthy foods bursting with vitamins, such as fresh fruits and vegetables, then you just went on a hunger strike until burgers, fries, and pizza appeared once more on your plate.

According to a scientific study by researchers from the University of Basel in Basel, Switzerland, elderly people who had higher blood levels of vitamin C and beta-carotene scored better on memory tests. The study involved more than four hundred men and women whose antioxidant levels were first tested in 1971. Twenty-two years later (in 1993), when they ranged in age from sixty-five to ninety-four, they were tested again, and subsequently given several standardized memory-related tests.

According to the tests, the people who scored higher on recall, recognition, and vocabulary tests were significantly associated with higher vitamin C and beta-carotene levels from the 1993 and 1971 blood tests. These results remained consistent even after the researchers accounted for age, education, and gender.

Although scientists said that this might be one of the first studies to examine the link between antioxidants and memory, they also discounted the use of antioxidant supplements as a factor in their results. Only 6 percent of those tested mentioned vitamin supplementation, and they did not show higher levels on blood plasma vitamins or better performance in the cognitive tasks. These studies are similar to another research effort in New Mexico, where people with the lowest levels of vitamin B_{12} and C scored badly on memory tests.

The bottom line? Eating the right foods rich with vitamins seems not only to provide health benefits, but memory benefits as well.

Tip of the Day

Does being tired influence your ability to remember? Of course it does, which is why it is never wise to practice committing things to memory when you're drowsy or just plain exhausted. Day 1 included a discussion on how one of the keys to having a good memory is paying attention, and that sometimes when people say "I don't remember," what they really mean is "I didn't pay attention." Obviously, paying attention is much more difficult when you are tired or rundown, and you cannot devote your full concentration to the information that you are receiving. Just like stress, cold medicine, sleeping pills, and other medications affect your memory, causing you to tire, so does just plain being tired affect it as well.

If you must remember something when you are tired, the best thing to do is to resort to one of the "old-fashioned" remedies, such as writing yourself a note or setting a reminder on a watch or electronic organizer. You could, of course, also ask someone to jog your memory with a reminder ("Say, Bill, remind me to ask Mr. Hodges about the Barnes account, will you?"). However, the danger here is twofold: The person that you're asking for the reminder could be just as tired as you, or they could be extremely forgetful as well.

The best thing to do when you feel so exhausted that your concentration is waning is to take a short nap, for about ten or fifteen minutes. Often this recharges your battery and helps you focus. If sleeping isn't feasible—if, for instance, you're at work and your boss frowns on you curling up on top of your desk—then try doing some relaxation exercises. Your memory will thank you for it! (For those that don't know, relaxation exercises can be anything from imagining yourself next to a cool mountain stream to sitting in a comfortable position. Check your local library or the Internet for more information.)

You've now reached the halfway point in this ten-day guide to sharpening your memory. If this were a horse race you would have just reached the midpoint of the contest. Don't falter now, because you're about to enter the home stretch—which starts with Day 6, where I'll continue the discussion of how you can use your new memory skills and tools for more everyday tasks.

Day 6

Using Your Memory Skills for Everyday Tasks, Part II

Remember in school when you occasionally asked the question "Why do I need to know this stuff? Once I get a job, will I really need to know President Warren Harding's middle name?"

If you found yourself asking that same question in the previous chapter when you were learning how to use those memory tools for remembering numbers, you'll find the answer in this chapter. Day 6 takes the information you learned in the last chapter and builds on it to introduce another important memory tool for learning numbers—phonetic sounds.

Words to Remember Things By

In the last chapter, you learned about how to use the Phonetic Number Code System to remember numbers. For the purpose of this chapter, I have repeated the consonant letters of this system.

0 = z, s (0 is zero)

1 = t (a "t" looks like a 1 with a line through it)

2 = n ("n" has two bars, just like a 2)

3 = m ("m" has three bars, just like a 3)

4 = r ("r" is the last letter in the word "four")

5 = l (in Roman numerals, "l" is the sign for 50)

6 = soft g or j sound and also ch and sh (6 resembles a capital "G")

7 = k (a "k" looks like a vertical bar)

8 = f, v (an "f" written in script has two loops, just like an 8)

9 = p, b (a 9 looks like a "p" reversed or an upside-down "b")

What follows is a challenging memory tool that uses this system to sharpen your memory.

What you're going to do with these phonetic sounds is create a library of words based on those consonant sounds. Sound confusing? It's not once you get the hang of it. Make sure you devise a simple word (and it's important that the word be simple, so it's easy to remember).

- The consonant sound for number 1 is "t." The phonetic word is "tie."

- The consonant sound for number 2 is "n." The phonetic word is "Noah," like the biblical figure.

- The consonant sound for number 3 is "m." The phonetic word is "Ma."

- The consonant sound for number 4 is "r." The phonetic word is "rat."

- The consonant sound for number 5 is "l." The phonetic word is "law."

- The consonant sound for number 6 is "sh." The phonetic word is "shoe."

- The consonant sound for number 7 is "k." The phonetic word is "key."

- The consonant sound for number 8 is "f." The phonetic word is "finger."

- The consonant sound for number 9 is "p." The phonetic word is "pie."

Now that you've run out of single-digit numbers, what do you do for double-digit numbers? For a two-digit number, the word must begin with the consonant sound representing the first digit, and end with the consonant sound representing the second digit. Even though that explanation sounds like a confusing phrase you'd find in a contract (such as "the party of the first part, herein referred to as the party of the second part . . ."), it's really not too difficult. Now let's list words for all the numbers up to 20:

- The consonant sound for number 10 starts with the "t" sound for 1 (the first digit) and ends with the "s" sound for 0 (the second digit). The phonetic word is "toes."

- The consonant sound for number 11 requires two "t" sounds for (1 and 1). The phonetic word is "tot."

- The consonant sound for number 12 is "t" and "n." The phonetic word is "tin."

- The consonant sound for number 13 is "t" and "m." The phonetic word is "tom-tom."

- The consonant sound for number 14 is "t" and "r." The phonetic word is "tire."

- The consonant sound for number 15 is "t" and "l." The phonetic word is "towel."

- The consonant sound for number 16 is "t" and "g" or "ch." The phonetic word is "touch."

- The consonant sound for number 17 is "t" and "k." The phonetic word is "tack."

- The consonant sound for number 18 is "t" and "f." The phonetic word is "tuft."

- The consonant sound for number 19 is "t" and "p." The phonetic word is "top."

- The consonant sound for number 20 is "n" and "s." The phonetic word is "nose."

Using the Advanced Phonetic Coding System

The next question in your mind is almost certainly: How is this coding system going to help my memory? The solution: Once you know these words, they will help you remember virtually anything, from a list of numbers to a random list of items, and they don't have to follow a particular order.

These phonetic words are used to help your memory. One way to look at the system is as a way to change the abstract—numbers—into something concrete. While it may be difficult to mentally picture the number 20, it certainly isn't difficult to picture the phonetic word—"nose." Once you become familiar with these phonetic words, then the image that the word suggests automatically pops into your head whenever you hear that number.

How does it work? Let's say, for example, that you need to remember ten items to buy at the grocery store and item number six is cheese. The phonetic word for number six is "shoe." Associate these two images in your mind with a visualization; a shoe made of Swiss cheese. If item number nine at the store is a mop, then associate this with the phonetic word for the number nine, which is "pie." Visualize yourself mopping up dozens of pies that have spilled on the floor.

You'll find numerous uses for this new memory tool. Say, for instance, that you have to memorize a number with many digits. Use your phonetic words and those pesky digits spring automatically to mind. Or say that you have to learn the fifty states in alphabetical order. State number 12 is Idaho, and your phonetic word for 12 is "tin." Thus, by using the substitute word tool, you come up with "Ida-hoeing" for Idaho. Now, visualize "Ida-hoeing tin"; see her straining at her hoe but instead of dirt she's digging up, it's shiny tin. Now it's easy to remember that "Ida-hoeing" is state number 12.

One of the advantages with this memory tool is how it's used to remember things out of sequence. Linking, for example, has its limitations: If you have twenty-five items on a list, and you need to remember item number 20, you would have to go through each item before you came to number 20. The same limitation is true with the loci method. To remember something that you've placed in your "bedroom," for instance, you'd have to make your way through your entire mental house until you came to the bedroom where you placed it.

Using the advanced phonetic coding system, however, alleviates these problems. Once you've devised and become familiar with your phonetic words, you will be able to remember any item on a list just by hearing its number, no matter what the sequence.

How many phonetic words should you know? That really depends upon your needs. Most people use this memory tool to remember a list of a hundred words. While that may seem long, once you remember the consonant sounds for each number, it's easy. Then, with a list of a hundred phonetic words, you're set when it comes to remembering anything from the fifty state capitals in random order, to the presidents in chronological order, to the three dozen items that you need at the supermarket.

Tool Time, Part 1: Phonetic Words for Numbers 21 Through 50

Now that you've gotten the idea of phonetic words and how to formulate them, devise a list that covers numbers 21 through 50. If you have trouble, below are suggestions to help you over the rough spots.

21. net	31. mat	41. rod
22. nun	32. moon	42. rain
23. name	33. mummy	43. ram
24. Nero	34. mower	44. rower
25. nail	35. mule	45. roll
26. notch	36. match	46. roach
27. neck	37. mug	47. rock
28. knife	38. movie	48. roof
29. knob	39. mop	49. rope
30. mouse	40. rose	50. lace

Times Are a-Changin'

Back in the good old days, it was fairly easy to remember television stations because they were just a handful in existence. (Don't forget, the television dial only used to go up to 13, and most areas didn't get all thirteen stations.)

Today, of course, things are radically different. Now a household gets dozens, even hundreds of channels, making it extremely difficult to remember which number corresponds to which channel. But fortunately, your memory tools can help.

Virtually all channels contain either two or three call letters; the trick is to turn the letters into a visualization that also triggers the corresponding number. For instance, let's say that HBO (Home Box Office) is channel 22 in your area. Use your substitute memory tool to come up with three new words for the letters HBO, such as Hairy Brown Ogres. Can you see the ogres, with their hook noses, beady eyes, and long brown hair? Now, to remember 22, try using your phonetic word for the number, which is "nun." Thus, to remember HBO, think of Hairy Brown Ogres chasing a bunch of nuns and you will remember that the channel number is 22.

Exercise: What Channel Was That Again?

Below are ten television station letters and their channel numbers. Come up with substitute words for each letter, and then use the appropriate phonetic word to remember the number. Then, use both in a visual.

1. TMC (Turner Movie Classics)—10

2. NBC (National Broadcasting Company)—7

3. CBS (Central Broadcasting System)—32

4. WB (Warner Bros.)—27

5. ABC (American Broadcasting Company)—14

6. TBS (Turner Broadcasting System)—39

7. TNT (Turner Network Television)—30

8. AMC (American Movie Classics)—64

How did you do? Here are some suggestions for the substitute words (the phonetic words you should already know):

1. TMC (**T**oo **M**any **C**ats and toes).
   Visual: Too many cats stepping on your toes.

2. NBC (**N**ew **B**oy **C**ashier and key).
   Visual: New boy cashier dropping his key.

3. CBS (**C**ows, **B**ears, and **S**heep and moon)
   Visual: Cows, bears, and sheep jumping over the moon.

4. WB (**W**alking **B**ottles and neck).
   Visual: Walking bottles with very long necks.

5. ABC (**A**ngry **B**lue **C**ar and tire).
   Visual: Angry blue car gets a flat tire.

6. TBS (**T**errifying **B**ig **S**nakes and mop).
   Visual: Terrifying big snakes squeezing a mop.

7. TNT (**T**iny **N**ew **T**iger and mouse).
   Visual: Tiny new tiger running away from a mouse.

8. AMC (**A**pple **M**arshmallow **C**ake and cherry).
   Visual: Apple marshmallow cake with a giant cherry on top.

Tool Time, Part 2: What Was the Number of That Banana?

Now let's practice using your phonetic words to remember items, without any suggestions. Below are items that you need at the farmer's market. Although you've numbered the items on your list, the way you encounter them in the market is different from your numbers. Use your phonetic words to remember each item out of your numbering sequence. Your reward, if you get this right, is that you won't have to go back out to the farmer's market and get those items you forgot!

1. Bananas

2. Green peppers

3. Corn

4. Tomatoes

5. Strawberries

6. Potatoes

7. Peaches

8. Eggplant

9. Onions

10. Squash

11. Plants

Exercise: Phonetic Words for Numbers 51 Through 100

Now it's time to devise a list for the last fifty phonetic words. Just in case you had trouble, here are suggestions:

51. lot	61. sheet	71. cat	81. fit	91. bat
52. lion	62. chain	72. coin	82. phone	92. bone
53. lamb	63. gym	73. comb	83. foam	93. bum
54. lure	64. cherry	74. car	84. fry	94. beer
55. lily	65. shell	75. coal	85. file	95. bell
56. leash	66. judge	76. cage	86. fish	96. peach
57. log	67. chalk	77. cake	87. fog	97. pig
58. leaf	68. chef	78. cave	88. fife	98. puff
59. leap	69. ship	79. cap	89. fob	99. pipe
60. cheese	70. case	80. vase	90. bus	100. disease

Open the Memory Tool Chest:
The Story Method

By now your memory tool chest is bulging with tools to help you remember everyday tasks. However, there's still some room left for another tool—the story method.

The story method is similar to the link memory tool. It relies on an interconnection between items, with the one prior triggering the next, and so on. However, the difference—as you've probably guessed—is that the story tool requires the creation of an entire story, rather than random words, phrases, or sentences.

You don't have to write the Great American Novel to use the story method. Any type of narrative that includes all the components that you need to remember will do the trick.

For example, let's say you need to pick up the following items at the supermarket: butter, eggs, milk, steak, cheese, potatoes, and bread. To remember them, you need to come up with a story, such as the following: The butter was driving the eggs into town when they saw the milk and steak having an argument over the cheese on the street corner while the potatoes and bread stood by watching.

The story method is limited by the amount of items that have to be remembered. Think of how long and complicated the story would be, for instance, if you had to remember fifty items. Researchers have found that the story technique is effective for remembering abstract words, and that nonrelated sentences are often remembered better when they're part of a story rather than just standing alone.

Exercise: A Story About Party Favors

You're planning your child's fifth birthday party and you need to buy treats for the goody bags. You know you want to buy the gifts at the toy store but don't want to waste time going down each aisle trying to remember what you need. Below is a list of five items for each gift bag. Use the story method to recall your list.

- Stickers
- Crayons
- Candy
- Noise makers
- Bubbles

How did you do? Here is one example.

The stickers and crayons ran around the candy store tooting their noise makers and blowing bubbles.

Pop Quiz: The Pen Is Mightier Than a Bad Memory

Below are eight errands you need to do. Using the story memory tool, make up a narrative that incorporates them all.

- Get car washed
- Return videos
- Buy stamps
- Fill your gas tank
- Buy bagels
- Have extra keys made
- Return library books
- Make pedicure appointment

Memory Sharpener: How to Become the Life of the Party

Say your business lunch conversation turns to art. When your clients can't remember what school of painting Picasso and Braque belonged to, you instantly chime in that they were cubists. How did you remember this, even though you read it in a magazine article months ago? By using your substitute word memory tool, you visualized a large cube with a breaking rock (Braque) and a pickax (Picasso). Perhaps you were even breaking the rock yourself with the pickax.

When the artists Monet and Renoir are mentioned, you immediately inform your companions that they were impressionists. While they marvel at your knowledge of art, you don't divulge that, once again, your substitute word memory tool provided you with the answer: In your mind's eye, you saw money (Monet) sliding down a runway (Renoir) while an artist painted an impression of each. When you read that Salvador Dali was a surrealist, you immediately pictured a dolly (Dali) that was so lifelike it was "sure real."

But why stop just at schools of painting? Who painted *American Gothic*? That's easy: Grant Wood. You know that because, once you read it, you used your substitute word tool to visualize the two farm folk in the painting standing next to large woods. Or how about the artist of *The Scream*? You announce, Norwegian artist Edvard Munch. You remembered that by picturing a monk standing calmly while someone is screaming nearby.

Do you see how using your memory tools opens up new horizons? You've gone from someone who couldn't remember his or her spouse's birthday to a person who can pluck artists and their styles out of your memory as if by magic.

Of course, you don't have to stop with art. Who wrote

Rabbit Is Rich? While your party guests might not know that the author is John Updike, you do, because you immediately visualize a rabbit running up a dike (Updike) while carrying a huge bag bulging with money. To think of the author of the horror novel *Salem's Lot*, visualize a king sailing (Salem) through parking lot after parking lot to remember that the writer is Stephen King.

How about music? To remember that Rossini composed the famous comic opera *The Barber of Seville*, visualize a rose growing out of your knee (Rossini) with very long hair that is being cut by a barber. What composer wrote *Swan Lake*? That, of course, is Tchaikovsky, which you knew because you visualized chives coughing on skis (Tchaikovsky) while skiing across a lake full of swans.

So the next time you're at a party, business lunch, or other social occasion, try using your memory tools to make a good impression.

Daily Tune-up: Remembering Weekly Appointments

How many times has this happened to you? You make an appointment—either for personal or professional reasons—but when the day and time arrive, you are doing something else, the appointment completely forgotten.

If you're tired of your family giving you the silent treatment for your forgetfulness or your having to make excuses to your boss about why you missed the meeting, then it's time to use your memory tools to remember your weekly appointments.

Of course, to remember errands, appointments, and so on for the next day, you simply use a link. If you have to go to the dentist tomorrow and buy butter on the way, link both together by having the dentist covered with butter. When you picture the dentist you can see the butter just dripping off him.

However, for many people the problem is remembering appointments or important dates that occur later in the week. By unleashing your memory tools, you will conquer this most vexing of memory problems.

The problem with remembering future appointments is the old one of how to remember something that is abstract: a day and time. By now, however, you know that the way to do this is to turn something abstract into something concrete. Fortunately, if you look in your memory tool chest you just happen to have the perfect memory tool for it—the phonetic word.

Phonetic Words

Here's how it works: Number the days of the week beginning either with Sunday or Monday, depending upon which is most logical for you. For the purpose of this explanation, let's say that you begin with Sunday, which would make that number 1, Monday number 2, and so on. Now, let's say that you have to pick up an important client at the airport at three o'clock on Wednesday. Since Wednesday is day number 4, you can turn the appointment into a two-digit number: 43 (4 for Wednesday, 3 for the pickup time).

So what's the big deal, you ask? It's just as hard to remember 43 as it is to remember Wednesday at 3:00. Normally, that is true—except that you have a phonetic word for 43: "ram." Now do you see where this is headed? Link the word "ram" with your appointment by visualizing a giant ram smashing through the glass front doors of the airport. See the ram with its huge, curved horns breaking through the glass; hear the glass as it shatters. Watch as everyone runs in terror from this unexpected visitor. If you make the image vivid enough, you should have no trouble remembering it, and what it stands for.

You can use this method for any appointment during the week. Monday at 1:00 becomes number 21, Tuesday at 4:00 becomes 34, and so on. By coming up with a visualization for each, you will remember each appointment. And, by the way, here's one instance in which those phonetic words from 51 to 100 that you came up with earlier will come in handy. For example, Friday at 7:00 becomes number 67—the phonetic word is "chalk."

Multiple-Digit Hours

There are a few exceptions to this method, such as how to take care of the double-digit hours 10:00, 11:00, and 12:00. For example, for a Monday appointment at 1:00, you would use the phonetic word "net" (for number 21). For Monday at 11:00, your first phonetic word is "new" (Monday is the second day of the week, so 2 is represented by "n") and your second phonetic word is "tot" (remember that number 11 is represented by two "t's" made into the word "tot"). Therefore, Monday at 11:00 is "new tot."

As far as whether or not the appointment is A.M. or P.M. it should be obvious; after all, lunch appointments don't happen at 12:00 A.M. in the morning. And finally, what if your appointment is not precisely on the hour, but in minutes— say, Monday at 2:15? Instead of driving yourself crazy by adding another phonetic word, simply use the words quarter, half, and three quarters to represent various parts of an hour (15 minutes past, 30 minutes past, and 45 minutes past). Then work this word into your visualization. In the example above, having the ram smash through the airport door while quarters are pouring out its ears like a slot machine should suffice to remind you that your appointment is not exactly at two o'clock, but 2:15. If your appointment is at, say, 2:20 or 2:40, pick up the nearest quarter hour *before* your appointment, so you won't be late!

Pop Quiz: Remembering Appointments

Below are five appointments that you have to remember for next week. (For the sake of this exercise, Sunday is considered the first day of the week.) Use the advanced phonetic coding system for each appointment, and then devise phonetic words and a visualization for each one.

1. Physical therapist: Tuesday at 3:00

2. Lunch with client: Friday at 1:00

3. Meeting with attorney: Tuesday at 9:00

4. Dinner with spouse: Friday at 6:00

5. Breakfast with accountant: Thursday at 7:00

Answers:

1. *Physical therapist: Tuesday at 3:00.* This translates into 33; the phonetic word is "mummy." A visualization of your dentist wrapped in bandages, just like some modern-day Boris Karloff, should do the trick.

2. *Lunch with client: Friday at 1:00.* This translates into 61; the phonetic word is "sheet." A visualization for this is your client hanging sheets out on the line to dry while a big table full of food sits off to the side, wrapped in a colorful sheet.

3. *Meeting with attorney: Tuesday at 9:00.* This translates into 39; the phonetic word is "mop." A visualization for

this is your attorney, dressed in custodial garb, mopping the floor outside his or her office or your office—wherever you have the appointment.

4. *Dinner with spouse: Friday at 6:00.* This translates into 66; the phonetic word is "judge." Picture your spouse dressed in a black robe, sitting behind a judge's tall desk and ready to pound the gavel and pass judgment on you.

5. *Breakfast with accountant: Thursday at 7:00.* This translates into 57; the phonetic word is "log." Picture your accountant trying to stay on a log floating in the water, while attempting to eat breakfast at the same time.

Exercise: The Game's Afoot!

Just to make sure that you've got the hang of this, let's try it backward. Below are four visualizations based on *suggested* phonetic words previously listed in this chapter. Put on your detective cap and try to figure out what time, and what appointment, the visualizations refer to.

1. A mop chasing your dentist around his office.

2. A lion sitting in the library reading.

3. A gigantic cherry perched on your son's head while he is playing soccer.

4. Dozens of cats running all over your grandmother.

Answers:

1. A dentist appointment on Tuesday at 9:00 (number 39, mop).

2. A 2:00 meeting at the library on Thursday (number 52, lion).

3. Picking up your son at the soccer field at 4:00 on Friday (number 64, cherry).

4. A visit to your grandmother's house at 1:00 on Saturday (number 71, cat).

Exercise: Remembering Birthdays and Anniversaries

In this chapter you've learned how to remember weekly appointments. The Phonetic Number Code System also applies to birthdays and anniversaries as well. Devise a visualization and phonetic word for these fictional dates.

1. March 22—your wife's birthday.

2. June 28—your parents' anniversary.

3. August 14—your nephew's birthday.

4. January 12—your daughter's birthday.

5. May 10—your grandparents' fiftieth anniversary.

Answers

- March 22
  Phonetic word for 22: "Nun"
  Visualization: A group of nuns "marching" (March) up and down the aisles in a church.

- June 28
  Phonetic word for 28: "Knife"
  Visualization: A brand-new knife with the name "June" engraved on the handle.

- August 14
  Phonetic word for 14: "Tire"
  Visualization: "A gust" (August) of wind blowing a tire swing back and forth in your backyard.

- January 12
  Phonetic word for 12: "Tin"
  Visualization: A note saying "Jan you are [January] in need of a new tin cup."

- May 10
  Phonetic word for 10: "Toes"
  Visualization: A manicurist saying to you, "*May* I paint your toes?"

Lessons from Mom: Stop Being a Couch Potato

If there was ever an award for saying one phrase more than any other during all the millions of words spoken between a parent and child, "Turn off that TV, get off the couch, and get some exercise" would almost certainly be the winner. How many times did your mother beg, plead, threaten, cajole, and even bribe you to get off your duff and get some fresh air? But you, in full training mode for the Couch Potato Olympics, would have none of that. Considering exercise second only to homework in activities to avoid, you consistently defended your right to become part of the furniture.

As it turns out, your mother was right. The positive benefits of exercise affect virtually every part of your body—including your brain and thus your memory.

Research has indicated that vigorous physical activity may get your brain up and running the same way it does your heart, while also improving creativity. The study found that women who jogged for two twenty-minute sessions per week were better able to devise alternative uses for everyday objects. Of course, since the key to coming up with these alternative uses is combing one's memory to find these uses, it stands to reason that exercise stimulates the memory as well.

Another benefit of exercise as a memory aid is that it often helps you relax and sharpen your focus. Many people suffering from stress find relief and relaxation in exercise. Since stress and anxiety have a negative impact on memory, it makes sense that as the stress dissipates, the memory function strengthens.

You thought your mother was just being a sadist when she kept harassing you to climb off the couch, go out, and get some fresh air and exercise. She thought she was trying to stop you from turning into a soft, lumpy pillow with eyes and a mouth. Little did you both know that your mother was trying to help both your body and your memory—and that she was right again!

Tip of the Day

Granted, there's a conspiracy out there against eating badly. Not only is eating the wrong foods bad for your health in so many ways, but now there is a growing body of evidence that eating right helps improve your memory.

Scientists know that the body needs the right amounts of nutrients, such as proteins, vitamins, carbohydrates, and lecithin, to keep essential chemical processes operating effectively. Among these processes are those that are vital to memory—registering, retaining, and remembering information.

However, since it's uncertain which foods specifically aid memory, most researchers agree that the best thing to do is simply eat a balanced diet, such as low-fat dairy products, whole grain breads and cereals, vegetables, fruit, seafood, lean meat, and poultry.

While more research examining the link between food and

memory is still in the early stages, there are some fascinating facts emerging. Choline, for instance, is a substance that appears to greatly impact memory. One study found that participants who ate foods rich in choline (organ meats such as liver, eggs, soybeans, and fish) showed an increase in acetylcholine, a brain chemical that functions as a neurotransmitter and is vital to memory. These participants were then able to recall a list of unrelated words more quickly than those who did not eat choline-rich foods.

Research also shows that if you need your brain to work at peak efficiency, such as for an important memory task, don't overeat. All that food sitting in your stomach takes the mind's attention away from the job at hand. A light meal, on the other hand, keeps your mind sharp and your memory unencumbered.

When you first picked up this book, the idea of having a sharper memory in ten days' time probably seemed like a pipe dream—like walking into the corner deli and picking the winning numbers for the lottery out of thin air.

But now you've completed six days, and you know that you can do it—you know that by using the tips and memory tools discussed in this book, you can improve your memory power. In Day 7, I will discuss how to remember facts and useful information such as directions, addresses, and telephone numbers. In addition, you'll encounter Mom again for some words of wisdom.

Day 7

Facts and Useful Information, Part I

I'm sure you can think of someone you know who refuses to stop to ask for directions when he or she is lost. Since there is no medical evidence to support the existence of a mysterious "nondirectional" mechanism in people, we might consider the reason is that they're afraid they'll forget the directions by the time they get back to the car. After all, nobody wants to suffer the indignity of asking for directions a *second* time.

Using some of the tools you've collected in your memory tool chest, you will be able to remember directions, addresses, and other facts and useful information without a problem.

Remembering Directions

Thanks to your memory tools, you're going to be able to remember directions as easily as names, faces, and numbers. The tools needed to remember directions are three of your most reliable: association, imagination, and linking.

The primary difficulty with remembering directions is that

too much unfamiliar and often repetitive information is fed into your memory at one time, so that all you remember are bits and pieces. Did he say make a left or right at the light? And by the way, which light was it? The third or the fourth? Does that include the blinking light coming up, or just actual traffic lights? By the time you try to sort all of this out, you're so confused you can barely remember how to drive your car, let alone the directions.

The chances are great that you have experienced the above scenario at least once, if not more often, in your life. But by using your memory tools, you don't ever have to be clueless on the road again.

The first thing to do when getting directions is to establish a peg. Remember that a peg is a familiar place where you file or put unfamiliar information. It's best to ask the person giving you the directions for a landmark. For example, if you are told to "go down four blocks, and after that take a left," you don't know how many blocks the person is counting: Is he starting with the one that you're on, or the next one? However, if you ask the person, "What's on the corner where I take the left?" and she answers "a pizzeria," then you know precisely where to take that left. The pizzeria becomes your peg.

Let Your Imagination Lead the Way

Now it's time to use your imagination. Another problem with getting directions is that "left" and "right" can get confusing. If you're told to take the "first left after you take the fourth right down past the third traffic light," it's almost guaranteed that you're going to confuse those numbers the moment you get back on the road. However, if you turn to your memory tools once again, what do you do when faced with remembering abstract concepts? You turn them into something concrete. In this case, you need to turn the abstract words "left" and "right" into something concrete and memorable. You have to choose the words that work best for you. For right now, you'll use "lambs" for left and "rabbits" for right. But, of course, not just a few lambs standing around looking bored, but a whole pack of lambs making loud noises, with their fur flying and heads bobbing. Use the same exaggeration technique for rabbits.

Now what do you think of when you hear the word "left"? That's right, lambs. And for "right"? Correct—rabbits.

So, instead of hearing "go down four blocks and after that take a left," you hear "go down to the pizzeria where you'll see a group of lambs." To firmly set this image in your mind, link the lambs with the building by having them swarm all over the pizzeria, running up and down the aisles, and helping themselves to pizza and soda. Once you get back on the road, even if you forget the number of blocks, or if it was a left or right, as soon as you see a pizzeria, the image of all those marauding lambs comes to mind, and you know it's time to make a left.

By using your memory tools of association, imagination, and linking, you've now conquered your fear of forgetting directions.

Tool Time, Part 1: Where Am I Again?

Now it's your turn. Use the memory techniques described above to change the four abstract directions below into a concrete visualization. For remembering numbers use the Phonetic Number Code System. In this exercise, continue to use "lambs" and "rabbits" for left and right. To help you come up with a visualization, I have provided a landmark for each one.

For example, you can remember "go down three blocks, past the intersection (gas station), and take a right," by translating it into: Go down marshmallow (3) blocks past the gas station and take a rabbit. To remember numbers in each example, you can use the Phonetic Number Code System.

1. "After the third traffic light, take a left at the stop sign (blue mailbox) and a right two more blocks down."

2. "Go down to the corner (the bank) and take a left. Go down about three blocks and make a right. After you pass a T intersection (bagel shop) and a blinking light, take the first right and then the second left."

3. "Take the first right on this road, then the second left. Cross the intersection (a park) and take the first left, then go two blocks down and take the first right."

4. "Take the third right after the stop sign six blocks down, after you come to the jug handle (bookstore)."

Exercise: Practicing Familiar Directions

Let's face it, it's always more difficult doing something the first few times. Why wait until you're hopelessly lost to try these memory techniques for remembering directions?

To give yourself more confidence with these techniques, practice them over the next few days. Think about directions that you know really well, such as how to get to your home or office, and use the memory tools to remember these directions as if you were hearing them for the first time. Remember, the more comfortable you feel using them, the easier they will be to use when you really need them.

Remembering Telephone Numbers

Think of how much time and effort you would save by being able to remember telephone numbers without having to look them up. Even storing the numbers electronically, such as in the phone's memory system, an organizer, or notebook computer, doesn't guarantee that they're always going to be at your fingertips. After all, batteries do go dead and machines do malfunction—usually when you need them most.

Instead of relying on other methods, it's better if you turn your memory into a giant telephone book where you can pluck any number that you need at any time.

Here are steps for remembering ten-digit phone numbers (including the area code):

1. Break the number down into manageable pieces, the same way you broke down long names.

2. Devise a visualization for each part of the number, based on the Phonetic Number Code System you learned in Days 5 and 6.

3. Link the visualization with the person.

For example, let's say you need to remember the phone number of your old friend Catherine Knott, the one with the pronounced chin that you met in Day 3. Since you already know Catherine, and can visualize her in your mind's eye, she becomes the peg onto which you can place the rest of the information. (If you're trying to remember the phone number of a company, you can create a visualization for the company using its name or perhaps the kind of business it is.)

Catherine's telephone number is 410-472-6291. By using the Phonetic Number Code System, you can turn "410" into "rts," "472" into "rkn," and "6291" into "gnpt." You now have to add vowels to turn these consonant sounds into words. The first word (the area code) becomes "riots," the second "raccoon," and the third "gunpoint." Thus, Catherine Knott's telephone number is "riots raccoon gunpoint."

Now that you've got the words, you can peg them to Catherine by using those old favorite memory tools, visualization and imagination. Visualize a riot of raccoons carrying guns, pointing them at some distant target with Catherine right in the middle of the group, acting as their squad leader. To make the image more memorable, picture the gun-toting rioting raccoons crawling on the ground commando style, with Catherine right there beside them, dressed in green battle fatigues. Now when you think of Catherine's phone number, the image of those rioting raccoons springs right to mind, and so does the phrase "riots raccoon gunpoint." By taking the vowels out of the words and reverting back to their phonetic sounds, you quickly come up with Catherine's number.

That's all there is to remembering telephone numbers. While at first it may seem awkward and time-consuming to convert the numbers to sounds, then words, and then come up with a linking visualization, you'll find yourself doing it faster and faster each time you practice it. Of course, the more times you call Catherine the more you'll remember her number, until finally you won't need the visualization at all. The number pops into your head as easily as if you had written it on a piece of paper.

Helpful Tips

Before you move to the exercise below for converting telephone numbers, here are a few tips to help you if you're having trouble with the consonant/vowel concept:

1. Insert vowels in alphabetical order—a, e, i, o, u. Don't immediately try to see what "ro" can be, for instance.

Start with "ra"; you can often save yourself a lot of effort.

2. Consider all the possible vowel combinations before deciding upon the best one. Sometimes, the first one that you find may not be the best or most memorable.

3. Remember that several numbers offer more than one option for consonant sounds. The number 8, for example, has the consonant sound for both "f" and "v." Don't get frustrated if your first attempt doesn't work.

Tool Time, Part 2: Number, Please

Below are five telephone numbers.

1. Break the numbers into their consonant sounds.

2. Convert the consonants into words by adding vowels.

3. Devise a visualization for each.

1. 122-3752

2. 380-7022

3. 041-7910

4. 641-9538

5. 562-7439

How did you do? Were you able to come up with concrete words and visualizations for each number? Just in case you had trouble, here are some suggestions:

1. 122-3752
   Consonant sound: tnn-mkln or "tin makes lunch."
   Visualization: A person made of tin, slapping together peanut butter and jelly onto bread to make a sandwich for lunch.

2. 380-7022

    Consonant sound: mvs-ksnn or "moves casino."

    Visualization: A shaking, rollicking gambling casino.

3. 041-7910

    Consonant sound: srt-kpts or "straight Cupids."

    Visualization: Picture a bunch of Cupids flying about in straight lines, aiming their tiny bows at whoever or whatever is your peg.

4. 641-9538

    Consonant sound: grt-blmf or "chart blue movies."

    Visualization: A large chart on which are the names of sad movies.

5. 562-7439

    Consonant sound: lgn-krmp or "Lincoln clear mop."

    Visualization: A tall, gangly Abe Lincoln vigorously mopping your kitchen floor.

Daily Tune-up: Political Strategies

Although politics may not be your cup of tea, it won't hurt you to know more about the individuals who make decisions about your future. If you want to see how easy it is to increase your political knowledge using your memory tools, I will show you how.

If you have trouble remembering the names of your senators and representatives, for example, use your substitute word tools to help you out. "Century," "centaur," or even "tore" work as a substitution for senator. Next, think of the names. For example, the names of the two New Jersey senators are Frank Lautenberg and Robert Torricelli. Since both of these are long names, break them into syllables according to their pronunciation: "lout-ten-burg" and "tor-ra-celli." Now think of visualizations for each one. For Lautenberg, you can use "out ten burgers," and think of ten hamburgers sliding into home plate in a baseball game and being called out by an umpire. To add the senator title, put the word "centaur" into the visualization, such as picturing the ten hamburgers riding on the backs of centaurs as they both slide into home plate. For Torricelli, use "tour-a-cell," and then think of centaurs touring jail cells at Alcatraz in San Francisco.

While most people don't have too much trouble remembering that they have two senators from their state (even if they can't remember their names), the number of congressional representatives is another story. Think quickly: Do you know how many congressmen there are, in total, from your state, and how many of them are Republicans and how many are Democrats?

It shouldn't surprise you to learn that your memory tools can help you remember this information. Let's visit New Jersey again, which has thirteen representatives: seven Democrats and six Republicans. First, use your phonetic number code to come up with a consonant sound for the numbers 7 and 6. Next, in order to differentiate between Democrats and Republicans, have the word that you come up with for the Democrats always end in "d," and the word for the Republicans always end in "r." For example, the word "kind" signifies the seven Democrats (the "k" sound from your phonetic code for 7, plus the last letter "d"). For the six Republicans, the word "jar" works (soft "g" or "j" sound from your phonetic code for 6, plus the last letter "r").

Once you have this system committed to memory, you can use it to remember the number of congressional representatives from any state. Don't forget to include a substitute word for the state and you're all set. To remember there are six congressional representatives from Oklahoma, associate "O.K. Homer" (Oklahoma) with a word such as "rag" (the "r" as the first letter signifies that it means "representatives," while the "g" sound is for the six representatives). For Oregon's five representatives, use "oar-gone" with "real" or a similar word.

Use this system to remember other political information, such as the number of state representatives for each state. In fact, you can even use this system to remember a state's electoral votes. To do this, you must choose a word that signifies electoral votes, such as a word that starts or ends with "e." For instance, Kansas has six electoral votes. First, come up with a substitute word or phrase for Kansas, such as "can sass," and then use a word that starts with "e" but contains the consonant sound of the number "six," such as "each." Thus, "can-sass-each" means to you that Kansas has six electoral votes. Come up with a visualization for "can-sass-each" and you're done. (Of course, the number of Congressional representatives and electoral votes changes according to a state's population, but let's not worry about that now!)

Exercise: Politics by the Numbers

Here's your chance to broaden your knowledge of politics in the United States. For numbers one through five below, come up with a substitute word for the state, and then a word to remember the number of congressional representatives for each one. If you want to make the exercise more challenging, you can include the number of Democrats and Republicans for each state. For numbers six through ten, devise a substitute word for each state, as well as a word to signify its number of electoral votes.

Congressional Representatives

1. Ohio—19 representatives
2. Texas—30 representatives

3. Wisconsin—9 representatives

4. Massachusetts—10 representatives

5. Florida—23 representatives

Electoral Vote

6. Colorado—8 electoral votes

7. Georgia—13 electoral votes

8. New York—33 electoral votes

9. Washington—11 electoral votes

10. Michigan—18 electoral votes

Lessons from Mom: Some Things Are Better Left Forgotten

Remember your first romantic breakup, when you thought your world was going to end? As you lay on your bed, crying your eyes out over being dumped, your mother brushed your hair softly and said, "You're better off forgetting him (or her)." Didn't your mother understand that you could never forget the first love of your life?

As it turns out, your mother was right. Sometimes people are better off forgetting. Chances are you immediately forgot the first love of your life when the second one came along. And if you didn't right then, you probably forgot about him or her as time went on. By concentrating on the present, most of us manage to forget painful memories from the past. This is a natural human reflex that most of us possess and that enables us to maintain good mental health.

It is a natural human trait to forget bad experiences. For example, there were probably many things that happened to you in school that made you feel terrible, but how many of them can you recall today? The less time you spend dwelling on negative memories, the more room you'll have to hold the necessary and positive information. Since stress inhibits memory, the less emotional clutter you have the more relaxed you'll be. So, even though it seems strange to say this in a book about increasing memory power, sometimes it is better to forget—just as your mother said.

Tip of the Day

You've almost certainly either seen or heard about herbal supplements such as ginkgo biloba that apparently improve your memory. But do they really work?

As with many natural remedies that have become popular recently, the jury is still out on the exact effects that herbal supplements like ginkgo have on boosting memory power. Ginkgo has become popular in recent years, following reports published in the media, including the *Journal of the American Medical Association*, that research had found potential for ginkgo in treating Alzheimer's disease, as well as in aiding memory.

Studies show that ginkgo improves blood flow to the brain by reducing blood viscosity. Research revealed that one third of Alzheimer's patients taking ginkgo showed improvement in tasks involving memory, such as remembering the date, daily activities, or the names of relatives.

Ginkgo comes from the ginkgo tree, a plant so primitive that it does not produce flowers but rather an unpleasant-smelling fruit. Despite its odorous offenses, the Chinese have long considered ginkgo to be a valuable aid in promoting longevity. Eventually word spread to Europe, where doctors now prescribe ginkgo extract in low doses for patients with circulatory problems.

Scientists caution that results of tests on ginkgo are too premature to draw any definitive conclusions. They point out that not all ginkgo products are the same, and that many do not contain all the active ingredients of those in formal studies. Memory loss can be triggered by a variety of conditions, such as depression or malnutrition, that don't respond to ginkgo. Of course, it's always best to consult with your doctor before taking any herbal supplements, especially if you currently take any prescription drugs. As to whether or not ginkgo biloba is a memory pill, it is just too soon to tell.

Now that you've completed seven days of this ten-day course in improving your memory, you should feel an immense sense of accomplishment. You've learned how to use your memory tools to help you remember things you never thought possible. While this book has helped you, all the credit should go to you: Your persistence and determination are the driving force behind your improvement.

There are just three more days left to go. In Day 8, you'll learn more facts and useful information, such as strategies to combat absentmindedness.

Day 8

Facts and Useful Information, Part II

Have you ever pushed your sunglasses up onto your head when you went inside, then, when you came back outside, couldn't remember where you had put them? Have you ever locked the car, started walking to where you were going, then suddenly couldn't remember if you had locked the car or not, forcing you to go back to check? How many times have you gone back home to see if you turned off the stove?

If you've ever done any or all of these things, then you, like so many other people, suffer from absentmindedness. Fortunately, you've come to the right place for a cure. Consider this chapter like a doctor's office for finding remedies for your absentmindedness.

Memory Sharpener: How to Combat Absentmindedness

In earlier chapters, the point was made that when you say you can't remember something, in reality what you mean is that you did not commit the information to memory in the first place. The same is true with absentmindedness; when you can't remember where you put your sunglasses, you think you're absentminded, but in reality you just weren't paying attention when you removed the glasses from your face. You didn't commit the location to your memory.

Usually, it's routine tasks that slip your mind. Why? Because the tasks stopped being interesting or unusual, making it difficult to focus your full attention on them. For example, if every time you turned off your stove it did something different—played a song, made a sound, spit out dollar bills, or said "Thank you," then it would be easier to remember to turn it off because the chore would not be routine, but varied. Routine blunts your attention and perception so that familiar things and tasks become unremarkable and invisible.

Another cause of absentmindedness is distraction. If you're thinking about the important presentation that you have to make at the office the following morning when you pull into your driveway, chances are slim that you're going to remember if you locked your car when you go inside the house. Quite often, people who daydream suffer from the inability to focus on the present. Instead of paying attention to the task at hand, you're thinking about tomorrow, and completely ignoring the present.

So now you know the why of absentmindedness. The big question is, what can be done about it?

First, let's address routine tasks. One strategy to overcome absentmindedness is to link the routine activity with something that won't slip your mind. For example, if each morning you forget to take your medication, make it a rule and part of your morning ritual that you will not get dressed until you take your medication. By doing this, the two tasks become connected in your mind, and you're less likely to forget to take your medication.

What helps you remember is order. Just as you learned that memory works better when you store information into mental file folders, the same holds true when you remember things in an orderly environment. For example, if every day you walk into the house and just put your sunglasses any old place, it's little wonder that you can't find them when you next want them. Designate a spot (dining room table, kitchen counter, and so on) for your sunglasses and every day lay them there. Make it part of your coming home routine: Come into the house, take off your coat, hang up your coat, and put your sunglasses in their proper place (this is good for keys, too). Eventually it becomes ingrained in your memory as part of a routine.

Exercise: Taking Inventory

How many times do you walk around your house trying to remember where you put things? The solution: Put each item back in its proper place. By doing this you will stop asking yourself, "Where are my glasses?" "What did I do with my keys?" Take an inventory of your house and find a specific place to keep the following ten items.

- Matches
- Candles
- Scissors
- Tape
- Coupons
- TV remote control
- Bills to be paid

- Checkbook
- Briefcase or purse
- Slippers

Occasional Tasks

Many absentminded people run into trouble remembering occasional tasks or activities. For example, every second Monday you're supposed to go to the library and volunteer. More often than not, however, the second Monday finds you and the library miles apart. Or, you walk into the house carrying a bill from the mail that is due in a week. You put it aside, telling yourself you'll pay it later, and the next thing you know, you've gotten another bill for the same thing, this time with a late fee on it.

Here are a few tips to remember occasional tasks:

- **Reminder notes.** If you know on Monday that you have to pay your quarterly taxes on Friday, write it down on a piece of paper and hang it in a place where you will see it, such as the refrigerator or bathroom mirror.

- **Make a general things-to-do list.** Devise headings for each day, and write down everything that needs to be done under the appropriate category. After you complete each task, cross it off the list.

- **Use visualization.** For instance, say you must be at the library every other Friday to help Mrs. Henderson, the librarian. To remember your appointment, visualize Mrs. Henderson somewhere that constantly reminds you of her. For example, if every night you use the microwave to cook dinner, picture Mrs. Henderson's face inside your microwave every time you open the door. Each time you prepare dinner there's Mrs. Henderson, frowning furiously at you, with a pencil behind her ear, sitting in the middle of your dinner.

Visualization, exaggeration, and humor tools also help you cure your absentmindedness in other ways. For example, say every time the telephone rings, you take off your glasses, then when you finish your conversation you can't remember where you left them. The next time the phone rings, visualize an image as you're putting down your glasses. If you leave them on the television, visualize a giant pair of glasses on top of the TV; add two huge eyeballs staring through the frames, blinking and looking all around.

If you're known for pushing your sunglasses up on top of your head and then forgetting about them, visualize a huge pair of sunglasses on your head every time this happens. They're so big, in fact, that they're weighing you down so that you're barely able to walk. This image helps you remember where your glasses are the next time.

In the morning if you want to remember that you brought your umbrella to work, visualize a place that you look at frequently, such as your computer. See your umbrella on top of the computer, dripping water all over your keyboard. At the end of the day, when you turn off your computer, the image of your umbrella springs to mind reminding you to bring it home.

Just Give Me Some Kind of Sign

Another way to combat absentmindedness is to give yourself a visual clue that a task needs to be done. The sign should be something out of the ordinary, so that it triggers your memory.

For instance, say that your mother-in-law is coming to visit on Thursday, and you must clean out the refrigerator before her arrival. However, with work, kids, and everything else, there is a real danger that you'll forget. To help you remember, take an empty box or container of perishable food, such as an egg carton or rinsed-out milk carton, and place it in a location where you'll keep seeing it, such as on the TV, on top of the bed—even in the middle of the kitchen floor. Now every time you see that carton out of place, it triggers your memory for the task at hand.

Using a visual clue like this is the same as those old tried-and-true methods of remembering, tying a string around your finger or putting a rubber band around your wrist. The trouble with relying on those oldies but goodies is that if you're truly absentminded, you're never quite certain what they mean. They are too abstract to be of much help. That's why a specific visual clue is far more effective. The more you encounter it, the better it works as a memory aid. For example, to remember to pick up the dry cleaning, hang an empty hanger on your front doorknob. Each time you go out you'll have to move that hanger, alerting your memory to your dry cleaning.

Tool Time, Part 1: Seeing Is Remembering

Here's something that is self-explanatory, but bears repeating: Visual clues only work if you use them when the task that you're afraid of forgetting is fresh in your mind. It's not effective to think, "Oh yes, I must make a visual clue to remember _____," and then go off and do something else and forget about both the task and making the clue.

The following exercise is similar to the old honor system of purchasing newspapers from a metal rack without a locking cover where you're trusted to put the appropriate change into the metal box before you take one. Over the next week, each time you know you have a task, chore, and so on, give yourself a visual clue to remember it. Continue devising visual clues until you no longer have to tell yourself to do it. Remember that you're on your honor to come up with a clue as soon as the task happens!

Why Am I Here Again?

Certainly you've had this happen to you: You walk into a room to get something, only to completely forget what it was, or even why you're in this room in the first place. If this happens to you all the time, there is hope: The good news is that you're not cracking up. It happens to everyone. The more frantic and busy our lives become, the easier it is to become so distracted that we can't even remember simple things from one second to the next.

The solution? Try this simple strategy. The next time you walk into another room to get something, stop before doing it and repeat to yourself what you are about to do: "I'm going into the bedroom to get a flashlight." Just as repeating a person's name out loud helps you remember it, so saying the task out loud prevents you from forgetting it. The benefit is that, even if you still walk into the bedroom and forget why you're there, you can retrace your steps to where you were when you stated the task. Often, just returning to that point helps you associate that particular spot with what you said, and you'll remember.

Improving Awareness

Although these hints and tips go a long way toward overcoming absentmindedness, none of them addresses the root cause of this condition: awareness. While this sounds relatively simple, the fact that people everywhere struggle with absentmindedness shows that it's not as easy as it sounds to lick. To improve your awareness, use the following procedure:

- **Pause.** Stop and think about your actions *before* you do them. By switching your mind from "automatic" to "manual," so to speak, you break the cycle of self-acting responses and force yourself to think about what you are doing. Before running out the door, or rushing into the next room, stop, pause, take a deep breath, and calmly ask yourself: "What am I doing?"

- **Concentrate.** It's not enough to think about what you are going to do if immediately afterward your thought patterns leap to an entirely different subject. Concentrate on what you are doing right now. Say it out loud to yourself: "I am going into the kitchen to see if I turned off the stove."

- **Anticipate.** Think about the obstacles that might deflect you from your task *before* they occur. If, for example, every morning you forget to take meat or fish out of the freezer for dinner because the instant you walk into the kitchen you check on your plants on the windowsill, then move your plants. By anticipating distractions you can take steps to deal with them. Does a display window at a department store grab your attention as you walk into work so that you forget to buy the morning paper? Take a different route to work. In the morning, do you forget to take your vitamins because you're making the kids' school lunches? Make the lunches the night before, or, better yet, make it a habit to take your vitamins before you pour your morning coffee, juice, or tea.

- **Act now.** No one knows if Benjamin Franklin was absentminded, but when he said, "Never put off until tomorrow what you can do today," he hit the nail right on the head. There is no substitute for immediately acting when you think of something, rather than putting it off. Do you need a book on classical music from the library to finish your report? Get it now. If you can't, then give yourself a visual clue, write a note, anything to remind yourself—just do it now. Do you need to pay the utility bill now? Then put it someplace where you'll see it and remember it.

Tool Time, Part 2: I Swear I Will . . .

Here is another "honor system" exercise. Resolve to yourself right now that today, when you get home, you're going to try becoming more aware. Use the first step in the above procedure and take time to pause and think about your actions before moving forward. After you have mastered pausing, then move on to the next step—concentrating. Don't be concerned if it takes a week, two weeks, or even longer before you feel comfortable with pausing.

Open the Memory Tool Chest: Spelling Tools

By now you should realize that your memory tools can help you in a variety of ways beyond just basic remembering. The more often you use these tools, the more you will realize how truly versatile they are.

For instance, did you know that memory tools help with spelling? That's right, spelling can be mastered through the use of tools and techniques that you've learned in this book.

Rummage around in your memory tool chest for two favorites: visualization and imagination. Now you've got spelling right where you want it.

Words with double consonants are among the most difficult to spell, such as "occasionally." To remember how to spell "occasionally":

- Visualize the word as bright red letters on a white background.

- Sound out the letters of the word.

- For the difficult part, devise a small phrase that triggers your memory, such as: "Mistakes sometimes *occur* when spelling *occasionally.*" The two "c's" in "occur" help you remember that "occasionally" also has two "c's" (and not two "s's").

Another method is to turn the word into a visual image that you'll remember. For the word "occasionally," think of two clowns going into a store and buying a soda. The one clown tries to drink it all, but the other one fights for his share using clown methods, such as squirting the greedy clown with seltzer. Next, link the image to the word with a phrase, such as, "Occasionally, two clowns will fight over one soda." The "two clowns" and "one soda" helps you remember that "occasionally" has two "c's" and one "s."

Let's try another. The word "commemorate" often drives people crazy because of all those "m's."

- Visualize the word as bright red letters on a white background.

- Sound out the letters of the word.

- Devise a phrase to help you remember the sequence of two "m's" followed by one "m," such as: "I *command* you to *come* here to *commemorate* this event." The two "m's" in "command," followed by the one "m" in "come," help you remember the sequence of "m's" in "commemorate."

To turn "commemorate" into a memorable visualization, picture two Marines and one Martian marching at the head of a parade with music, flags, and floats. The Marines are an impressive sight in their dress uniforms, while the Martian has one eye, is green, and rather unattractive. The phrase that links this word with the image is, "Two Marines and one Martian are commemorating the first visit by an alien to Earth."

Exercise: Words to Remember

Below are thirty-five difficult words to spell. Use your memory tools to help you remember the correct way to spell each.

1. accumulate	13. notorious	25. quorum
2. affirmative	14. obsequious	26. rhythm
3. fulsome	15. catacomb	27. bimillenary
4. souvenir	16. hippopotamus	28. versicolor
5. title	17. innocuous	29. miscegenation
6. calendar	18. impatiently	30. subpoena
7. cataclysm	19. jewelry	31. tarantula
8. chlorophyll	20. laryngitis	32. precipitation
9. dessert	21. unctuous	33. vernacular
10. eclectic	22. millennium	34. concordance
11. essential	23. neurosis	35. garrulous
12. fluorescent	24. psychiatrist	

Daily Tune-up: How to Avoid Misplacing Things or People

How many times have you wandered around the parking lot at the mall looking for your car? Worse yet, how many times have you called mall security because you couldn't find your car, and then felt foolish as you drove around with the security guard trying to locate it? Here's what to do:

Pay attention to where you've parked. What stores are nearby? What other types of buildings are nearby? Are there any landmarks, such as trees, power lines, light poles, and so on? Come up with a visualization so that the image stays alive in your mind. Perhaps you can see the tree crashing down on your car or maybe you see your car poking through the giant "S" in a store sign.

Place it in one of your mental file folders. In Day 4, you created mental file folders based on the furniture in your living room. Let's say that you parked your car in Section 2. Your second living room mental file folder was "television." In your mind, create an image of your car sitting on top of your TV. This triggers Section 2 in your mind. If the parking section has a letter, such as "2B," then you can add another image to your visualization, such as "two babies." Picture two babies crawling all over your car while it sits on top of your TV. When you come out of the mall, the image of your TV and those crawling babies is all you need to help you remember "2B."

Your memory tools help you remember other types of information as well. Let's say that you've just started a new job in a large, multistory office building, and you need to remember that your human resource officer has an office on the sixth floor. Here's what to do:

- Make a note of any landmarks or visual aids to help you remember the location. Perhaps the office is right beside a water cooler.

- Devise an image of the person dripping wet, or even swimming in a tiny boat inside the water cooler.

- Place the image in one of your mental file folders that corresponds to six; if it's your house folder, then number six is the grandfather clock. Picture this person dripping wet sitting on top of your grandfather clock, and the image helps you remember that Human Resources is on the sixth floor, next to the water cooler.

Exercise: Now Where Was That Again?

Below are ten examples of people and things whose location you need to remember. Use your memory tools to come up with a method to remember the location for each.

1. Your car is parked at the mall in Section 5G.

2. Your wallet is on the kitchen counter next to the bread box.

3. Your briefcase is in the den beside your desk chair.

4. You hid a birthday present in your closet behind your shoes.

5. You put the extra fuses in the toolbox next to the electrical tape.

6. The conference room in your new office building is on the third floor, adjacent to the office supply closet.

7. Your hotel room number is 315 at the conference you're attending.

8. Your grandmother's apartment is number 645 on the ninth floor of the east wing at the retirement community.

9. Your boss's office is on the second floor, in the corner near the coatroom.

10. You've placed your address book in your second desk drawer, right-hand side.

Lessons from Mom: What Date Was That Again?

When you were going to school, and thought you knew so much more than the teachers, you undoubtedly felt that memorizing important historical dates was a waste of time. "Who needs to know this stuff?" you'd say. "How is knowing the date of Pearl Harbor Day going to help me in my future career?"

Your mother, of course, had an opposing viewpoint. She told you that you'd never know when that type of knowledge would come in handy. So she'd make you study those dates— no matter how loudly you complained.

As you have undoubtedly learned through the years, it does indeed pay to know certain historical dates. Of course, this doesn't mean that you have to know something obscure such as the day the ninth president of the United States, William Henry Harrison, died after being in office for just thirty days. However, if you're making a professional presentation on a date that has historical significance such as the day the Declaration of Independence was signed, for instance, it's both impressive and a good icebreaker if you open by commenting on the date. It's also important to remember dates so that you have a historical perspective on events and occurrences. For instance, if you're reading a newspaper on December 7 and there are several stories about modern-day Pearl Harbor in Hawaii, it helps to know that December 7 is the day Japan bombed Pearl Harbor rather than just thinking that the stories are running purely by coincidence. By the same token, if you have a friend who is a Kennedy assassination conspiracy believer, you may want to steer away from political conversations revolving around November 22—the day President Kennedy was assassinated in Dallas.

Fortunately, you already possess the memory tools required to remember important dates. To remember months, think of a word that recalls each month for you; for numbers, try using the symbol method. Let's give it a try with December 7, 1941—Pearl Harbor Day. To remember December, think of Santa Claus, while to recall 7, think of its symbol, which is a gallows (see Day 5). The symbols for 1941 are, respectively, a spear, snail, sailboat, and spear. So to remember December 7, think of Santa Claus sitting on top of a gallows. For 1941, think of a spear sticking through a snail that is lying in a sailboat . . . on top of another spear! To link this to Pearl Harbor Day, devise a humorous visualization; perhaps a beautiful, sun-drenched harbor that contains shiny white pearls instead of water. On the dock is a gallows with Santa Claus, while gliding on the pearls is a sailboat with snail and spears.

Now you try it. Below are four important dates in history.

1. June 6, 1944—D-Day
2. April 14, 1865—Lincoln's Assassination
3. December 26, 1620—the Pilgrims land at Plymouth Rock
4. April 9, 1865—Lee surrenders to Grant at Appomattox Court House, ending the Civil War.

Tip of the Day

One thing that Mom probably didn't tell you about studying—most likely because she wasn't aware of it—was to use a memory technique called PQRST. This method has proven to help people remember facts better.

PQRST is an acronym that stands for the five steps involved in this memory technique: preview, question, read, state, test.

1. **Preview.** Briefly look over the material that you need to learn in order to get an overview of the subject. Read the introductory paragraphs, the picture headings, tables, charts, and so on. In addition, if the material has a summary, read that first. This gives you a strong idea of the main points.

2. **Question.** Ask yourself questions about the information, such as, "What points is the material trying to convey?" and "What people are involved?" If you're reading a textbook, often you can find out the main points by first reading the review questions at the end of the chapter.

3. **Read.** Completely read the material without taking notes. The work you've done in the first two stages should help your understanding and comprehension. After you read the material once, go back and reread it, this time taking notes and underlining or highlighting the main points.

4. **State.** Speak out loud the answers to your key questions. Ask yourself more questions as you reread the chapter; state out loud the information that you've underlined or noted.

5. **Test.** Give yourself a test to make sure that you have retained and comprehended the critical points. Test yourself several times, staggering the tests each time. This helps you feel confident that you've grasped the information.

In Day 9, I will discuss how you can use your memory tools to remember recipe ingredients, items to bring on a camping trip, and personal traits of guests at a dinner party.

Day 9

Practical Memory Challenges

Your brain is always in a state of constant motion trying to recall several different things at the same time. Sometimes your memory becomes clouded by everything you have to accomplish during a day, week, or month. This chapter focuses on how you can apply your memory tools in everyday situations, from remembering a piece of information about a guest at a dinner party to remembering types of wines.

Opening the Memory Tool Chest: Practicing Visualization

Of course, a tool is only as good as how well you use it. So now it's your turn to practice using visualization to remember names and faces. Put a spit shine on your imagination tool by coming up with visualizations for the following first and last names, remembering to use humor and exaggeration whenever possible. Remember no visualization is wrong, as long as it works for you.

Tool Time Quiz: Putting Visualization in Your Tool Belt

Okay, let's get busy. Using your visual skills, come up with a visualization to remember the following six names.

1. Jim Applebaum
2. Wendy Donaldson
3. Frank Fletcher
4. Susan Moorer
5. Elliott Roberts
6. Gretchen Sterling

How did you do? Good. Just in case you were stumped by any of them, here are some suggestions:

1. Jim Applebaum
   Link: "Gym" for Jim, "Apple Bum" for Applebaum.
   Visualization: An apple dressed in tattered clothes (for instance think of Emmett Kelley's famous hobo clown), begging at a gymnasium.

2. Wendy Donaldson
   Link: "Windy" for Wendy, "Donald Duck's son" for Donaldson.
   Visualization: A pint-size version of Donald Duck being blown around by a strong wind, which can be visualized as one of those corkscrew-tornado images often seen in cartoons.

3. Frank Fletcher
   Link: "Hot dog" for Frank, "Fetch her" for Fletcher.
   Visualization: A hot dog that resembles a dog, complete with large eyes, panting tongue, and wagging tail, fetching a newspaper or pair of slippers.

4. Susan Moorer

   Link: "Sioux" for Susan, "Moor" for Moorer.
   Visualization: A beautiful Indian princess, dressed in classic Native American costume, wandering about on a dreary, foggy moor in the best tradition of Sherlock Holmes.

5. Elliott Roberts

   Link: "Yell a lot" for Elliott, "Robbers" for Roberts.
   Visualization: A robber, complete with black mask and unshaven chin, yelling and shouting like a spoiled child because he can't find anyone to rob.

6. Gretchen Sterling
   Link: "Great chin" for Gretchen, "Silver" for Sterling.
   Visualization: A gleaming piece of sterling silver with a proud, haughty face, and an oversized chin in the manner of Jay Leno.

Pop Quiz: Names and Faces for $500

Now it's your turn again. Below is a link, visualization, and facial feature or distinguishing characteristic for five people. All you have to do is supply the mental picture.

1. Chilton
   Link: "Chill ton."
   Visualization: A very cold one-ton weight.
   Characteristic: Prominent chin.

2. Graham
   Link: "Gray ham."
   Visualization: A rather disgusting-looking gray-colored ham, perhaps with a thermometer in its mouth and sad eyes to indicate its poor condition.
   Characteristic: Baldness.

3. Nussbaum
   Link: "Nose bum."
   Visualization: An extremely large proboscis (that's a
   fancy word for nose) dressed in hobo garb, perhaps even
   with a battered derby or Fedora on top.
   Characteristic: A very bright, flowered scarf.

4. Terranova
   Link: "Terrible nova."
   Visualization: A nova (an explosion in outer space)
   dressed in some really tacky, clashing clothes, and
   possibly with a wild hairstyle to match.
   Characteristic: Thick, connecting eyebrows.

5. Webster
   Link: "Web stir."
   Visualization: A spider perched happily in the middle
   of its web, using one of its eight legs to stir a pot of
   food.
   Characteristic: Hollow cheekbone.

How did you do? Remember, there are no right answers for
this exercise, so if you came up with a mental picture for each
one, congratulations.

Visualization Exercise: Days of the Week

Over the course of a week you have at least one important
task to accomplish daily. Below is a list of seven items you
need to remember for each day. Devise a visualization for each
one.

1. On Sunday, bring tulips to your weekly visit to Mom's
   house.

2. On Monday, dress your child in a purple shirt for Purple Day at her preschool.

3. On Tuesday, bring your raincoat to the dry cleaners so it's ready for your business trip at the end of the week.

4. On Wednesday, buy flannel sheets during the linen sale at the department store.

5. On Thursday, bring your bike to the repair shop for new tires.

6. On Friday, buy an ice cream cake for your co-worker's birthday.

7. On Saturday, buy blueberries for your famous blueberry pancakes to serve your spouse breakfast in bed.

Were you successful? In case you had trouble, here are suggestions for two of the seven items.

Purple Day on Monday: Visualize Barney, the purple dinosaur, dancing around your child's closet singing, "It's Monday, that means Purple Day," to remember to dress your child in a purple T-shirt.

New tires for your bike on Thursday: Visualize a bike with two flat tires trying to ride around the word "Thursday" on your day planner.

Top Ten List: Wine Connoisseur

If you're hosting a business lunch or dinner, and someone suggests that you order a bottle of white wine, would you know what to do, or would you just smile and nod your head? Some people know if a wine is a red or white simply by its name. For others, this poses more of a challenge. In business and social circles, whether or not you drink, it is handy to have a basic working knowledge of wine—and your memory tools can definitely help.

To avoid a sticky situation, here is a "cheat sheet" to help you remember ten of the most popular types of red and white wines, as well as their distinguishing characteristics. The first five wines are red, and the second five are white:

Red Wine

1. Beaujolais
   Characteristics: A wine meant to be drunk young; fruity, like strawberries.
   Visualization: Imagine a child (for young) named Bo (for *Beau*-jolais, pronounced bow-zhe-LAY) holding a basket of juicy red strawberries.

2. Cabernet Sauvignon
   Characteristics: Oak, green peppers, vanilla.
   Visualization: Picture a cavern (for Cabernet) filled with oak barrels stenciled with green peppers and vanilla beans.

3. Merlot
   Characteristic: Slightly sweet, cooked cherries.
   Visualization: Imagine the word "Merlot" spelled out with bright red cherries, cooking in a giant cauldron of boiling water.

4. Pinot Noir
   Characteristics: Slightly burnt plums or ripe berries.
   Visualization: Picture a pint (for Pinot) of plums or berries in a pot boiling over on the stove, filling the kitchen with smoke.

5. Zinfandel (not to be confused with white zinfandel, which is a sweet blush wine)
   Characteristic: Slightly sweet, red fruit.

Visualization: Imagine that you're making a large gift basket of "zin"-fully (for *Zin*-fandel) sweet red fruits such as luscious strawberries, tying it all up with a big red bow.

White Wine

6. Chardonnay
   Characteristics: Oak, grapefruit rind, pineapple, vanilla.
   Visualization: Imagine a dancing Carmen Miranda wannabee named Shari (for *Char*-donnay) with a big hat decorated with grapefruits and pineapples, licking a vanilla ice cream cone.

7. Gewürztraminer
   Characteristic: Perfume.
   Visualization: Picture a wine bottle filled with fragrant perfume stuck right in the middle of a big liverwurst (for Ge-*wurz*-traminer).

8. Reisling
   Characteristic: Perfumy fruit.
   Visualization: Imagine a bottle of wine resting (for Riesling) in a giant bouquet of fragrant white flowers.

9. Sauvignon Blanc
   Characteristic: Fresh cut grass or, alternately, melons.
   Visualization: Imagine you and a loved one savoring (for Sauvignon) a delicious picnic, sitting on a white blanket (for Blanc) on an expansive lawn of freshly cut grass.

10. Sémillon
    Characteristic: Hazelnuts.
    Visualization: Picture a half- or "semi"-bottle (for Sémillon) of white wine sticking out of the top of a truckful of hazelnuts.

Recipe Ingredients

You probably never considered using your memory tools to remember how many eggs go in a quiche or how much butter is needed for your favorite Christmas cookies. But as you will learn shortly, you can use humor, visualization, and substitute words to recall recipe ingredients.

Exercise: How Much Sugar Was That Again?

It's your turn to bring dessert to your neighbor's monthly pot luck dinner. This month you want to bring your mom's famous apple pie. However, you can't remember how much sugar to add and your mom is away on vacation. You don't want that to happen again. So think about your favorite recipe and devise a way to remember each ingredient and the quantity required using the memory tools you've learned so far. For example, let's get back to Mom's apple pie and how much sugar you need. Let's say you need one cup of sugar—visualize a one-cup measuring cup circling around your bag or canister of sugar.

Filing Information Away

You can use the system of creating mental file folders for a variety of tasks in your professional, personal, and social life.

Exercise: Creating Other Mental File Folders

Here's an exercise in which it's up to you to get creative. Find five other things (actually, sets of things) from which you can create mental file folders. The first one—items in a room in your home—has already been given to you in Day 4.

After you figure out what to use, practice making the folders. If you find that you prefer using one of these new folders rather than the body parts file folders, that's fine. Here are some suggestions: items in your kitchen, basement, office, garage, bedroom.

Repeat Exactly After Me

Although it won't happen too often, there are going to be times when you need to remember something that you read verbatim. Fortunately, your memory tools work in these cases as well.

The secret to remembering something written word for word is to break it into small pieces and then visually think about it. Since you have already done this for long numbers, the techniques and memory tools used are familiar.

Famous Lines

In Day 1, you were asked to use visualization to remember a passage. Here is your chance again. For example, let's say that you have to remember Thomas Jefferson's famous line from the Declaration of Independence: "We hold these truths to be self-evident, that all men are created equal, that they are endowed by their Creator with certain unalienable Rights, that among these are Life, Liberty and the pursuit of Happiness."

Strong words indeed, but quite a lot to have to remember verbatim. Fortunately, the passage is written in such a manner that it almost divides itself into shorter segments. Below is one suggested way of breaking this sentence up. The key points are on the left, with the remainder of each section in parentheses:

- We hold these truths (to be self-evident)
- Men (that all men are created equal)
- Creator (that they are endowed by their Creator)
- Rights (with certain unalienable Rights)
- Life (that among these are Life)
- Liberty (Liberty)
- Happiness (and the pursuit of Happiness)

It's important that as you break the sentence up, you repeat it aloud, word for word. Now let's think of visualizations for each section.

- **We hold these truths:** You hold in your fists a bunch of "truths" in front of a judge in a courtroom. You're holding the words by their first letter, "t," and the rest of the words are hanging down below. Therefore, you're holding truths for evidence.

- **Men:** All the jurors are men, and they all look the same, so they're all equal. To help increase the vividness of your visualization, make the men distinctive-looking, perhaps giving them a beard, mustache, thick eyebrows, a large nose, glasses, and so on. As you create these pictures, repeat the part of the sentence that you're working on word for word.

- **Creator, Rights:** Visualize what you have always thought your Higher Power looks like. The Creator is sitting at a desk in the courtroom *writing* with a long, green pen that's shaped like an alien—thus the key points "Creator" and "unalienable Rights."

- **Life, Liberty, Happiness:** In the courtroom on the wall behind the judge are three words in large red letters: Life, Liberty, and Happiness. But these words aren't just standing there lifeless—Life and Liberty are running after, or pursuing, Happiness. You can see the little cartoon clouds of white smoke under their feet as they run.

Now link everything together: In a courtroom you are holding truths for evidence before a jury of equal men, while the Creator "Rights" with an unalienable pen and Life and Liberty pursue Happiness. If you've used your imagination to make the visualization come alive in your mind, then the picture is extremely vivid.

If you prefer, you can use another memory tool, your mental file folders, to remember the above information. Put each main point—the equal men, the Creator writing, and so on—into its own file folder.

Now that you have the main points of Jefferson's famous sentence visualized, and you have also been saying each part out loud verbatim, you can repeat it word for word. Try doing that now.

Suddenly, it doesn't seem like such a mouthful anymore, does it? You can use this technique and your visualization, imagination, and linking (or file folders) memory tools to remember any written information verbatim, such as lines from a poem, passages from novels or plays, and so on. The secret is to break down long sections into shorter ones and then devise visualizations for each. Once you link the visual images together, the remainder of the passage will be triggered in your memory.

Applying the Loci Method

As we've seen, the oldest known mnemonic strategy is the loci method. Remember, this method is effective because it allows you to use familiar locations to remind yourself about things you want to recall.

Pop Quiz: Home Sweet Loci

Below are ten locations from your office building; the numbers in parentheses represent the order you encounter them each day. Also listed are ten points that you want to make in your upcoming speech to the board of directors. Match the points of your speech with the locations, using the loci method, and on a separate piece of paper describe how you visualize each.

Locations

- Front door (1)
- Security counter (2)
- Elevator (3)
- Water cooler (4)
- Hallway (5)
- Washroom (6)
- Your desk (7)
- Coffee machine (8)
- Secretary's desk (9)
- Supervisor's office (10)

Speech Points

- Welcome (1)
- Company overview (2)
- Acknowledgment of visiting representatives (3)
- Performance of existing products (4)

- New products (5)
- Profit and loss statement (6)
- Competitive overview (7)
- Examination of global markets (8)
- Personal views (9)
- Conclusion (10)

Practice Drill: Remembering Things to Bring on a Camping Trip

You're packing to go camping and you don't want to forget anything. To remember your gear, use the loci method and put each item in a specific location in your house. Try it on the following eight camping items: tent, stove, kerosene, lamp, compass, canteen, flashlight, sleeping bag.

How did you do? Here are some suggestions: Start at your front door, with the tent, and visualize the door covered by your camping tent. Next, enter the house and go into the living room. On the wing chair, visualize your portable stove, on the coffee table see a large container of kerosene, and on the couch, visualize your lamp. Next, move into the kitchen: Can't you see your compass attached to the front of your refrigerator, your canteen sitting atop the toaster, and your flashlight perched on the counter? Finally, in your bedroom, visualize your sleeping bag folded in the middle of your bed.

Memory Sharpener: Remembering Addresses

At this point you've learned how to memorize telephone numbers and directions. But what if you need to remember a person's address? Can your memory tools be used to remember a combination of numbers and words?

The answer, of course, is yes. Remembering an address involves using several of the memory tools you've already tucked away in your memory tool chest.

Combine Phonetics and File Folders

Let's say that you need to remember the address "49 Pleasanton Avenue." Remembering the number 49 is easy, because you've already devised a phonetic word for it: "rope" (remember from Day 6). So the question becomes, what should you link rope to? You've also previously answered this question as well, because you've already devised mental file folders of familiar things where you can store unfamiliar information. Remember the mental file folders you made out of your body parts? Here's an occasion to use them. The first file folder you made was your head, so picture the rope on your head. Perhaps it's wrapped around your head like a turban or it's just one limp piece of rope lying across your head. Either way, place "rope" into your head file folder. Now you've got 49 taken care of.

Take the Word Apart

The next component is the street name: "Pleasanton." If you rummage around in your memory tool chest, you'll find that you also have the means to remember this as well. You handle it the same way you did long names, by breaking it into syllables. Fortunately, Pleasanton breaks up easily into "pleasan" and "ton." Now you have to visualize images to go with these words. How about "pleasing ton"? Picture in your mind a large, one-ton weight (you know it's one ton because it says so on the side) that's pleasing in appearance. Perhaps it looks debonair, with a handlebar mustache and dark, flashing eyes. Or maybe it has the face of a famous movie star you love to watch on the big screen.

Link Everything Together

Once you've conjured up the visualization, the final step is to link everything together. Maybe you can have the rope holding up the pleasing ton with the face of Mel Gibson, or perhaps the rope is wrapped around the weight so that all you can see is Mel's handsome face. No matter how you do it, however, you have successfully changed the very abstract "49 Pleasanton Avenue" into a memorable, concrete visualization that helps you remember that address.

As you can see, all the tools necessary to remember addresses were already in your memory tool chest. This is also the case if the street number is greater than 100—just turn the number into consonant sounds using your Phonetic Number Code System, then turn the consonants into words by adding vowels. If you want to add the type of street (avenue, boulevard, and so on) or even the city to the address, you merely need to follow the same steps that you did to remember the street name.

After you use your memory tools a few times to remember addresses, you decide which technique or combination of techniques works best for you. Once you find tools that you're comfortable with and that work for you, stick with them. Before you know it, going through all the steps that you just did above will become second nature to you.

Tool Time: Do You Know the Way to . . . ?

Use your memory tools to commit the ten fictional addresses below to memory. Remember to use whichever tools you find work best for you.

1. 23 Farnsworth Avenue—your lawyer's office.

2. 77 Sunset Strip—your sister's new address.

3. 148 Philadelphia Avenue—where you send your college loan payment.

4. 265 Dromedary Lane—the address of your dream home.

5. 1035 Jersey Boulevard—where you have to take your child for piano lessons

6. 1449 Witherspoon Street—where your best friend just moved.

7. 46 Bramble Way—where you have to drop off your résumé.

8. 1114 Gowdy Street—the location where you were involved in a motor vehicle accident.

9. 59 Mulberry Place—where the florist is sending your order of roses.

10. 3428 Kensington Boulevard—the restaurant where your high school reunion is being held.

Exercise: City to City

Below are the names of ten United States cities that you will visit on your cross-country trip. Use your memory tools to devise ways to remember each.

1. Los Angeles

2. Chicago

3. Philadelphia

4. Des Moines

5. Houston

6. Boston

7. Tallahassee

8. Raleigh

9. Charleston

10. Spokane

Lessons from Mom: Stay with Your Buddy!

Do you remember class trips? Trips to historic sites, parks, businesses, and other places were one of the highlights of any school year, mainly because you got out of school.

When the trips took place in elementary school, you were always assigned a "buddy"—a person you had to stick with like glue throughout the trip. The theory was that it's far easier for one kid to wander away than two, so each of you looked out for the other. If you were lucky, your buddy was a friend, and everything was fine. If you were unlucky, your chosen buddy was someone you did not like, and you spent the whole trip in misery at being chained to that person.

Complaining to Mom about this sad state of affairs was useless; in her mind there was safety in numbers, and so she just told you to hang with your buddy and enjoy yourself. You, of course, were convinced that she didn't have a clue about the horror you were going to have to go through.

It turns out, however, that she was right: Having a buddy *is* a good idea, particularly in the case of your memory. Sometimes when people live alone they become more forgetful. While this is partly because there isn't anyone else to stimulate their mental faculties, another reason is that having another person around is like having a second memory. How many times have you said to your co-worker, spouse, or friend, "Don't let me forget to ___"? If you're both trying to remember the same thing, then a buddy doubles your chances of not forgetting. You can use your memory buddy for a variety of tasks—everything from reminding you to call the electrician to remembering to buy a birthday present.

Daily Tune-up: Remembering Personal Traits

People enjoy being flattered, especially in a business or professional setting where every little advantage helps. Fortunately, your memory tools provide you with the perfect opportunity to offer just the right bit of flattery to someone by remembering a personal trait, hobby, or some other remark that he makes in passing. While others let that information idly slip by, you remember it and use it to make a good impression.

How can you do this? Simple. By linking the trait, activity, hobby, or whatever you want to recall to the visualization you have already created for that person. For example, let's say you meet Joe Smith at a professional function and during the course of the conversation he mentions that he enjoys waterskiing. Now, the way you've chosen to remember Joe's last name is by linking it with "blacksmith," and the visualization is Joe standing in front of a large anvil in a blacksmith's shop. To add waterskiing to the image, just imagine Joe on water skis in his blacksmith's shop—a ridiculous image, granted, but one that is unusual enough to stick in your memory so that the next time you see Joe, you can impress him by mentioning something interesting or newsworthy about waterskiing.

Exercise: Match Game

Now it's your turn. Below are the names of nine people you've just met at a dinner party. Although you're going to get their names via business cards and write a polite thank-you note, you also want to include a trait, hobby, or additional piece of information that you obtained at the party to make the note more personal. Each person's distinguishing feature and a piece of additional information is listed. Come up with a visualization for each that enables you to remember their name and trait. (For the sake of this exercise, assume that you've already come up with a visualization to remember the name.)

1. John Bigelow
   Feature: Large nose.
   Trait/hobby: Learning to fly a plane.

2. Randi Sears
   Feature: Big blue eyes.
   Trait/hobby: Loves gardening.

3. William Judge
   Feature: Bright sweater.
   Trait/hobby: Just returned from Rome.

4. Sarah Masterson
   Feature: Big glasses.
   Trait/hobby: Likes old movies.

5. Carl Peterson
   Feature: Prominent front teeth.
   Trait/hobby: Plays golf.

6. Donna Briscoe
   Feature: Always wears scarves.
   Trait/hobby: Scuba diver.

7. Terry McNulty
   Feature: Mustache.
   Trait/hobby: Collects matchbooks.

8. Brenda Jackson
   Feature: Long, thin fingers.
   Trait/hobby: Enjoys opera.

9. Alan Ackerman
   Feature: Beard.
   Trait/hobby: Hockey fan.

Time's up! How did you do? Below are some suggested answers.

1. John Bigelow
   Visualization: Planes landing and taking off from his large nose.

2. Randi Sears
   Visualization: A bevy of colorful flowers blooming all around her eyes.

3. William Judge
   Visualization: Roman gladiators fighting it out all over his bright sweater.

4. Sarah Masterson
   Visualization: Humphrey Bogart, Clark Gable, Marilyn Monroe, and other old-time stars sitting on her glasses frames.

5. Carl Peterson
   Visualization: A golf club and balls, and the numbered flags for each hole all sprouting out of his front teeth.

6. Donna Briscoe
   Visualization: Skin divers and tropical fish swimming happily up, down, and around her scarf.

7. Terry McNulty
   Visualization: Matchbooks sticking out of his mustache.

8. Brenda Jackson
   Visualization: Opera performers in full costume scampering up and down her fingers.

9. Alan Ackerman
   Visualization: Hockey players poking their heads out of his beard.

Tip of the Day

If you want your brain and memory to function better, tell them both to "go fish."

In Day 4, we talked about the importance of fish in helping a child's brain develop. But fish helps not just kids; your memory can be aided by it too, just like the exercises in Day 9 help give you a sharper memory.

Recent studies indicate that the omega-3 fatty acids in fish such as salmon create new communication centers in the brain's neurons, which promotes optimal brain function as well as mood. According to the results of one study, men who ate three quarters of an ounce of fish daily reduced their odds of contracting age-related memory decline by 60 percent, as compared to study participants who didn't eat fish. Indications are that one portion of fish oil known as DHA (docosahexaenoic acid) seems to enhance the power, speed, and efficiency of the brain, as well as provide these same benefits to both memory and learning. Researchers are also checking on the ability of omega-3 fish oil to treat Alzheimer's disease, depression, and schizophrenia.

You don't need to eat an ocean of fish to reap the benefits of this amazing substance, either. Just a couple of servings, or an ounce or two daily, is sufficient to keep your brain and memory as sharp as a shark's tooth. Fatty fish, such as mackerel, sardines, and herring, are all great sources of omega-3 oil. And if fish isn't your favorite, taking approximately 650 milligrams per day of omega-3 (DHA) and EPA (eicosapentaenoic acid) in capsule form will do the trick.

In Day 10, I will talk about how to use your memory tools to help your reading comprehension and to remember stock market symbols, among other final helpful hints. There's also one final lesson from dear old Mom.

Day 10

Tips, Memory Boosters, and Summary

Isn't it annoying when you read something over and over again, but can't seem to make heads or tails of it, even though there are no unfamiliar words to contend with and the sentences are clear and well structured?

What's happening, of course, is that while the words and sentences may make sense to you, your comprehension is faulty. You just can't grasp the point that the writer is trying to make.

Fortunately, your memory tools can help solve this problem for you, as well as assist in several other areas in which you might not have thought they could prove useful. So, for the last time, sit down, open up your memory tool chest, and get ready to go to work.

Top Ten List: The Best Ways to Boost Your Long-Term Memory Skills

By now, you have a variety of tools and methods to sharpen and enhance your memory. However, there are also things you can do over the course of your life to try to ensure that your memory hums along at peak efficiency.

- **Pay attention.** It sounds too simple, but it's true. The more you pay attention, the more information you retain.

- **Keep a diary or day planner.** If appointments still bedevil you, keep a diary and write down each and every appointment as you make it. Put the diary in the same location each time so that you always know where it is.

- **Use all your senses.** Notice people and objects using all your senses, not just your eyes. For example, the slight burning smell your drip coffeemaker gives off when you leave it on after you have finished the coffee in the pot. Or the sound your child's humidifier makes when there is no more water left in the machine.

- **Relax.** Take your time, breathe deeply, and gather your thoughts before doing something. Every day doesn't have to be a pressure-cooker, because stress and anxiety wipe out memories as easily as erasers wipe clean a blackboard.

- **Don't overtax yourself.** Under the heading of "self-fulfilling prophecies," if you're worried about forgetting something, then that's almost certainly what will happen. Don't try to remember dozens of things at once.

- **Eat right.** Eating sugary, fatty foods is not going to enhance your memory. A balanced diet that includes the proper amount of vitamins, minerals, and protein helps your body, mind, and memory function better.

- **Drink water.** Aside from diet, drinking water also helps maintain your body's many systems at peak efficiency.

- **Get sleep.** Maybe when you were younger you could burn the candle at both ends, but no more. At this point in your life, your brain needs sleep for your memory to function effectively. Research indicates that during certain periods of sleep, the brain disengages itself from the senses and turns its attention to the memory—reviewing, processing, and storing information. If the brain doesn't get these opportunities, memory ability is affected.

- **Energize your surroundings.** Your memory thrives on variety; use different colors, shapes, and objects to energize your life and your memory (but make sure not to go to the other extreme and overload your senses).

- **Be positive.** Make life an adventure. Look on the bright side, and embrace the tremendous amount of diversity the world has to offer. That's the best way to help your memory stay sharp and focused throughout the years.

Teach Your Children Well

Children, as has often been stated, are our most precious resource. Therefore, it makes sense to explore ways that you can help your kids (or nieces and nephews) enhance and maximize their memory power, so that they avoid some of the memory problems that adults encounter.

Here's the good news: Even if your child is in high school, you can still take steps to enhance his or her memory skills. Research indicates that from birth through age twenty-five, memory follows an ascending curve. At twenty-five, it peaks, and remains at this level (barring illness or injury) for years, until age-related decline sets in.

Unlike adults, who sometimes think that they're too grown

up to think of silly visualizations, young children love using their imagination. It takes little prompting to get a child to concoct the sometimes far-fetched, often humorous visualizations that are at the heart of many memory tools and strategies. At the very least, young kids prefer to think visually. They may not know what a serpent is, for example, but if you tell them that it's like a large snake, it's likely that an image of a snake pops into their heads.

When the time is right, have your child use his imagination to think visually. Have him remember people, places, and things not by name, but by visual images. Make a game out of it by competing with him to devise the most outrageous visualizations possible. The more skilled that he becomes in learning how to think and remember visually, the better and more comfortable he'll be using this technique to maximize his memory abilities as he grows older.

You can also introduce several of the memory tools you learned, such as links and substitute words, to your children. For example, these techniques come in handy when you are trying to teach your child to remember everything they need to put in their backpack for school each morning.

Only you can know when your child is ready to benefit from some of the memory techniques. The key is to take it slow; don't get discouraged if your child doesn't show interest, and, above all, don't demand too much of either your child or yourself. By laying down a solid foundation when your kids are young, you may make lasting inroads that will still have an impact when they are older and wiser.

Summary Exercises

So you think you remember most of what you've read so far? Now's your chance to prove it. The following four summary exercises each contain five questions. When you've finished all four exercises, return to this scoring chart to see your ranking: 5 or fewer correct answers—It's back to the memory drawing board for you; 6–10—Your memory is faltering; 11–15—Your memory is alive and well; and 16–20—You're a memory marvel. Below is the first summary exercise: five multiple-choice questions about your memory tools.

Summary Exercise 1: Multiple-Choice Memory Tester

1. What does the loci method use as a memory aid?
   a. Familiar locations
   b. A story
   c. A peg word
   d. A person's occupation

2. How does linking work?
   a. By devising a phonetic word to go along with an image
   b. By placing a name with an image
   c. By devising mental file folders
   d. By substituting a familiar word for an unfamiliar word

3. What are mental file folders?
   a. Familiar places where you can store unfamiliar information
   b. Very small manila folders that fit inside your brain
   c. File folders you label with chores
   d. Personal characteristics that you can use to remember names and faces

4. Using "Indian-at-poles" for the city "Indianapolis" is an example of what memory tool?
   a. Loci

b. Imagination
c. Linking
d. Substitute words and phrases

5. What name is commonly given to memory tools?
   a. Memory tools
   b. Mnemonics
   c. Things to help enhance memory
   d. Memory Aids

ANSWERS: 1 c, 2 b, 3 a, 4 d, 5 b

Summary Exercise 2: Name That Name

Below are five uncommon names. Come up with a link and visualization for each one. Suggestions for each follow the exercise.

1. Cortelli

2. Gennello

3. Novatkoski

4. Riordan

5. Sugarman

Answers:

1. Cortelli: "Core-tell-Lee."
   Visualization: An apple core telling off Robert E. Lee, the famous Confederate general from the Civil War.

2. Gennello: "Gem-yellow."
   Visualization: A bright yellow jewel.

3. Novatkoski: "No-vat-cow-skis."
   Visualization: A cow skiing down the side of a huge vat and holding up a big sign that says "no."

4. Riordan: "Rear-Dan."

Visualization: A large parade of people, with a group of men that all look the same and are all wearing signs that say "Dan" around their necks bringing up the rear.

5. Sugarman: "Sugar-man."
   Visualization: A man made entirely of sugar.

Summary Exercise 3: What Was the Number of That Number?

For the first three numbers below, use the picture code to turn each into an image. For the last two, use the Phonetic Number Code System to create a visualization.

1. 567
2. 124
3. 938
4. 921-5320
5. 3446300

How did you do? Just in case you got stuck, here are some suggestions:

1. 567: A spread-out hand covering a snake that's swinging on the gallows.
2. 124: A spear through a swan lying in a sailboat.
3. 938: A snail sitting on a pitchfork that's sticking through an hourglass.
4. 921-5320: Pnt-lmns, which is "punt lemons."
5. 3446300: Mrrjmss, which is "mirror jams."

Summary Exercise 4: A Mixed Bag

Here is a potpourri of skills you learned throughout the ten days. Use your memory tools to answer each question.

1. Use your memory tools to remember how to spell "inadmissible."

2. How would you use your memory tools to remember the address 32 Reichert Street?

3. What are the phonetic words for numbers 36 through 42?

4. What are the phonetic words for numbers 81 through 87?

5. What is a good way to remember to perform occasional tasks?:
   a Leave a visual clue
   b. Decide that the task wasn't that important anyway
   c. Tie a string around your finger
   d. Get someone else to do it.

How did you do? Just in case you had any problems, here are some suggestions:

1. A visualization to remember that "inadmissible" is spelled with two "s's" and three "i's" is two *snakes* crawling into three *igloos,* with the phrase "It's *inadmissible* for two *snakes* to crawl into three *igloos.*"

2. Convert 32 to its phonetic word "moon." Break Reichert up into two syllables and come up with a substitute phrase: "rye-court." The visualization is a large, full moon shining down on a tennis court filled with pieces of rye bread.

3. In order, they are: 36 match, 37 mug, 38 movie, 39 mop, 40 rose, 41 rod, 42 rain.

4. In order, they are: 81 fit, 82 phone, 83 foam, 84 fry, 85
    file, 86 fish, 87 fog.

5. The answer is "a."

Lessons from Mom: Don't Get So Upset

She may not have said it to you when you were a child, but
you almost certainly heard your mother saying it at one time
or another to an older family member: "Don't get so upset.
You're going to raise your blood pressure and that's bad for
you." Blood pressure? To you, the only pressure that you
knew or cared about was the one that inflated the tires of
whatever vehicle you used to gain your freedom (first a bicy-
cle, then later a car). So you let your mother's words go in one
ear and out the other. You didn't take them to heart as you got
older, and watched your blood pressure creep up. You may be
wondering why this is in a memory book. High blood pressure can't have anything to do with memory, can it? It can.
Recent studies have indicated that high blood pressure speeds
memory loss in older people.

High blood pressure has long been identified as a risk factor in stroke and heart disease. But a decades-long study involving more than 3,700 Japanese-American men (although
scientists feel that these findings are just as likely to apply to
both genders) found that the participants with high systolic
blood pressure during midlife were almost two and a half
times more likely to have poor cognitive function in old age
than men with low systolic pressure.

According to researchers, the higher the blood pressure in
midlife, the greater the likelihood of suffering trouble thinking and remembering in old age. Statistics indicated that for
every ten-point increase in systolic blood pressure, there was a

corresponding 9 percent increase in the risk of poor cognitive function later in life. The subjects' cognitive function, which includes remembering, abstract thinking, making judgments, and concentrating, was measured when their average age was seventy-eight.

Daily Tune-up: Reading Comprehension

When people complain that they can't remember what they've read, they're being too hard on themselves. At the risk of oversimplification, there are two basic types of reading: for pleasure and required. Reading for pleasure is precisely that: a leisure activity. It is something you do at a particular time because it's what you want to do for relaxation or enjoyment. Whether it's a novel, newspaper, magazine, or the back of a cereal box, when you read for pleasure you're not actively trying to retain the information for long-term use. In some respects, reading for pleasure is similar to a conveyor belt: The information flows into your memory at one end, and then flows out the other, being replaced by new information at the receiving end. There is no motivation or necessity to retain this information.

Required reading is a different story. Whether it's for work, school, or elsewhere, when you do required reading you have a distinct purpose in mind, such as: "I must remember this material for the big presentation tomorrow." Because you are specifically trying to retain information for later use, you are motivated to remember it.

If you are having trouble remembering required reading, your visualization, imagination, and substitute word memory tools help out by turning words into easy-to-remember pictures. As an example, consider the following fictitious newspaper article below that you need to remember for a journalism class:

> *Today, Russian and British scientists discovered a new species of dinosaur outside Moscow. Called Canineosaurus, the small, doglike vegetarian creature apparently lived 40 million years ago and roamed from Russia all the way to China.*

First of all, since what the article is discussing is centered in Moscow, use your substitute word tool to change Moscow to "mossy cow." Now picture both Russian and British scientists riding that strange-looking cow, with green moss all over its body. Perhaps the Russian scientist has a goatee and a monocle, while the British scientist is wearing a pith helmet. What's walking alongside them? Why, a dinosaur, of course—a dinosaur with the face and body of a dog (for *"Canineosaurus"*), but with a dinosaur's reptilian feet and long tail. Can you see the face of the dog, panting happily, its tongue hanging out of its mouth, as it trots alongside the mossy cow and its two passengers on its huge dinosaur feet? Can you also see the piece of celery sticking out of his mouth (to indicate its vegetarianism)?

Now for the second part of the article. If you remember, you devised phonetic words for numbers up to 100, and the phonetic word for 40 was "rose." So now you have the mossy cow, its passengers, and the doggie dino walking on a path that contains nothing but millions and millions of roses—40 million, to be exact. In fact, they're not just walking on this path, but "rushing" (Russia). Why are they rushing? Because up ahead is a large table with china plates filled with food. Thus, the newspaper article above has been turned into the following visual image: "Two scientists on a mossy cow and a doggie dinosaur eating celery are rushing toward china on a path made of 40 million roses."

Although it may seem like it takes so much time to make

these visualizations that you could memorize the article in a shorter period, in reality by now you should have become so proficient at using your memory tools that these are coming to you almost instantly. It just takes a long time to explain them.

Another strategy to help you remember required reading is summarizing the material as soon as you read it, then commenting about it. For the above article, you could summarize it as: "Outside Moscow, Russian and British scientists found a vegetarian dinosaur resembling a dog that lived 40 million years ago and roamed from Russia to China." Repeat this summary a few times, commenting to yourself about it after doing so. Talk about it with a friend. The more you repeat and comment on it, the more solidly it remains in your long-term memory.

Exercise: Words to Pictures

The next time you read a newspaper, pick five short articles or news summaries and turn the words into pictures using your substitute word, visualization, and imagination memory tools.

Exercise: Summarize Time

After you're done turning those five articles into pictures, summarize them in one sentence. Repeat each summary several times, and discuss each article with another person. After a few days have passed, see how much of each article you remember.

Tip of the Day

Let's face it, most people are dabbling in the stock market today. Thanks to the Internet, you don't even have to go to a broker's office to get involved in the market; you can do it right from the comfort of your own home, via your computer.

Playing the market isn't easy, of course, and it becomes even harder if you have a faulty memory. There is a lot of information to remember—prices, company names, stock symbols, and so on—and even the smallest mistake can result in a big financial loss unless your information is both accurate and complete.

Fortunately, your memory tools also help you in your quest to become a Wall Street tycoon or even if you just want to make a couple of extra bucks on the side. There are three key elements to remember with stocks: price, the company name, and the company's stock symbol or abbreviated designation. Let's look at each more closely.

- **Price.** Use your Phonetic Number Code System to turn the abstract numbers into a visualization that you can see in your mind's eye. For example, if the stock is selling for $40.17 per share, the word "rustic" is a close phonetic equivalent. Here's why. The phonetic word for 40 is "rose" and the phonetic word for 17 is "tack."

- **Company names.** Substitute a word or phrase to represent the company. For Ford, an image of one of the company's cars that you're familiar with, such as a Mustang, fits. If you don't know any of the cars, then changing "Ford" to "lord" might help, since you can visualize an English lord, complete with powdered wig and frilly shirt.

  Since stock prices usually are expressed in fractions, you can either choose to ignore the fraction, or change the fractions into a visualization. You do this by converting all fractions to eighths, which is the common denominator used for all stock fractions. Then you use your phonetic words to remember the price. If, for instance, the Ford stock price was 40⅜, then the phonetic words that spring to your head are "rose Ma"—"rose" being 40, and "Ma" being 3.

- **Stock symbols.** The Ford is fairly easy—FordMot—but still abstract enough to cause potential problems. Using the substitute word memory tool, "FordMot" can become "Floor Mop." Now you've got the image of an English lord, dressed in his aristocratic finery, carrying a floor mop in the midst of a beautiful rustic scene. To others, "rustic lord floor mop" may sound like sheer nonsense but to you it means "Ford Motor Company at $40.17 per share."

Exercise: Price Pictures

Now that you've learned yet another way in which your memory tools are used, let's try an exercise to make the lesson stick. Below are five fictitious stock prices of companies. Use your memory tools to convert these prices to visualizations.

1. Transporter Computers: 37⅛. Symbol: TRSC.

2. Burning Speed Processors: 72⅜. Symbol: BrnSp.

3. Lakeland Automotive: 22⅜. Symbol: LKLD.

4. Celulex Office Supplies: 42⅞. Symbol: CLX.

5. Waterfun Pools: 14⅜. Symbol: WatPls.

Wrap-up

The memory tools in this book have helped you enhance your memory, and have shown you the way toward improving it even more in the weeks and months ahead. Although initially you may have doubted that *anything* could ever help your so-called bad memory, by now you have learned that there are, indeed, many tools, techniques, and procedures to help you remember things that you never thought possible.

So congratulate yourself. The old you, the one that couldn't remember names, faces, important dates, numbers, and numerous other things, is gone. The new one has both the tools and the knowledge to remember all those things, plus much more.

About the Authors

The Princeton Language Institute, based in Princeton, New Jersey, is a consortium of language experts, linguists, lexicographers, writers, teachers, and businesspeople that develops easy-to-read self-help books in a nonacademic format for writers, businesspeople, and virtually anyone who wants to enhance his or her communication and language skills. It is the creator of the *21st Century Dictionary of Quotations, 21st Century Grammar Handbook,* and *Roget's 21st Century Thesaurus,* which alone sold over one million copies.

A professional writer, journalist, and editor for more than fifteen years, Russell Roberts has published nine books and more than 200 stories and articles on business, travel, history, health and fitness, personal profiles, and special interest topics. He has extensive experience covering small business start-ups and management, franchising, and work-at-home opportunities. His work has appeared in dozens of newspapers and magazines including *USA Weekend, The New York Times Magazine, Chicago Tribune Magazine, Business Digest, Parenting, Americana, Art & Antiques, Military History, The Star-Ledger* (Newark), and *New Jersey Monthly.* He is the author of *Stolen, Discover the Hidden New Jersey, Down the Jersey Shore, Endangered Species,* and *All About Blue Crabs and How to Catch Them.* Russell Roberts resides in Bordentown, New Jersey.

The Philip Lief Group is a Princeton-based book developer in Princeton, New Jersey, that produces a wide range of language and usage guides including *Grammar 101, Guide to Pronunciation,* and *Roget's 21st Century Thesaurus.* The Philip Lief Group has been singled out by *The New York Times* for its "consistent bestsellers" and by *Time* magazine for being "bottom-line think tankers."